The Spirits Are Subject Unto You

Erica Shepherd

Integrated Healing Prayer Ministry

Every since the fall of Adam, there
Has been a Spiritual battle going on, for the possession of men's Soul's and Spirit's. There is
a Spiritual being named Satan who is also described in The Word of God as Lucifer or an
Angel of Light. And no wonder! For Satan he transforms himself into an Angel of Light. 2
Corinthians 11:14. There is also of course, The Holy Trinity of God, namely God the Father,
God, The Son and God the Holy Spirit. The Spirit filled Believer who has committed him or
herself to The Lord Jesus Christ as Lord and Savior has the indwelling presence of these three
persons of The Godhead. Our Bodies are intended by God to be The Temple of his Holy Spirit,
which comes to us when we yield ourselves to the Lordship of Jesus Christ and willfully
surrender to Him and His Will. "Do you not know that you are the Temple of God and that the
Spirit of God dwells in you? If anyone defiles the Temple of God. God will destroy him, for the
Temple of God is Holy, which Temple you are. 1 Corinthians 3: 16,17 and again" Or do you
not know that your body is the Temple of The Holy Spirit who is in you, whom you have from
God, and you are not your own? For you were bought at a price; therefore glorify God in your
body and in your spirit, which are God's. 1 Corinthians 6:19, 20.

The Spirits Are Subject Unto You

*Satan is not the source of all our problems, our sin is the largest contributing factor. In fact, leaning on our own understanding and working in our own strength also contribute to a large percentage of our problems. Once we begin to experience the consequences of fleshly and sinful decisions that we have made, our enemy is right there and suggests to our thoughts that it is God's fault for letting it happen, it is someone else's fault or we are losers and misfits that do not deserve to have any victories in life. The enemy will urge us to move fast to rectify the situation before things become worse and then before we realize it we end up digging ourselves a deeper hole than before. The enemy may even reveal himself to some during this period in order to paralyze them with fear because he is involved and trying to destroy them. Looking objectively at the whole scenario, many of the problems originated because of a lack of focus on the word of God in the first place, (seeking His guidance) and then the problems accelerated even greater because focus on the Word of God was not established during the crisis. The enemy will go out of his way to keep a person's attention on the problems, the circumstances or the enemy, so that people will not turn to their real source of strength, the Lord God. Focusing on God after a number of problems have developed is not always easy. Thoughts are racing through the mind, there is a great deal of anxiety, there is much confusion and distraction and frankly, you do not feel very spiritual at that moment in time. But this is when it is crucial to stop everything, step back to get a more objective view of the circumstance and then begin to follow the principles that God has revealed in His word. Paul's advice to the Philippians in chapter four can be of great help at this time. "Rejoice in the Lord always; again I will say, Rejoice." (4:4) In other words, begin to celebrate the Lord, for He is greater than any problem that we can face. Even though you may not feel like it, you must direct your faith to the character and attributes of our God. He is loving and compassionate (He cares), He is all-knowing and all-powerful. He is full of grace (unmerited favor) and mercy. Begin to "rejoice in Him." "The Lord is near." (4:5) He is near because His Spirit is in those who have received Jesus as Savior. He is near because He has promised to hear and answer those who trust Him and obey His commands. (Jn 15:7) He is near because He will not leave us to fend for ourselves. (Heb. 13:5) "Do not worry about anything. . ." (4:6) First of all, what will worrying accomplish? Secondly, worry shows that we are not trusting the Lord to help us. Choose to trust Him no matter what happens. Is not our faith in Him more important than possessions? How long will our possessions last us anyway? They are insignificant in comparison to eternity.". . . with thanksgiving let your requests be made known to God." (4:6) Thank God for who He is, for Jesus' sacrifice, for the victory we have in Jesus, for the Holy Spirit that has been given to us, for the promises that God has given us, for God's faithfulness to us in the past and for the future we have with Him forever.. (Spend time praising God - it may be difficult in the circumstances, but if you will persevere, the freedom to praise will come.) Praise will empower your prayer. It will increase your faith. It can renew your strength and help you see God's perspective. And praise can put Satan on the run! After you have praised and thanked God, make your requests known to God. Present your case to Him. Let Him know what you want, why you want it and how it will bring glory to Him. "And the peace of God, which surpasses all understanding, will guard your hearts and your minds in Christ Jesus." (4:7) Now wait for God's peace to come. He has promised that He would guard your hearts and minds with it. Most people finish their time with the Lord before His peace comes. If you have to wait fifteen minutes, a half-hour or more than an hour, wait until it comes. It will be worth it!!! Many have missed this blessing because they were anxious to see something happen or to do something. But if His transforming peace does not come, you will not fully be prepared for what God wants to do with you from that point on. **It is this biblical process that our enemy wants to keep us from. He will press us to do something now so that we do not get a chance to "rest in the Lord.". . . Let us throw off everything that hinders and the sin that so easily entangles, and let us run with perseverance the race marked out for us. Let us fix our eyes on Jesus, the author and perfect or of our faith, who for the joy set before him endured the cross, scorning its shame, and sat down at the right hand of the throne of God."** *(Heb 12:1-2)*

Erica Shepherd
Integrated Healing Prayer Ministry,
Exorcism, Healing, Deliverance, Inner-healing
TED, Line, Inc. Live Telephone Exorcism Deliverance
805 ½ Geneva Street
Opelika, Al. 36801
1-877-230-1110-Office
334-460-9972
Email:
erica@phonethetedline.com
http://integratedhealingprayerministry.com
http://Phonethetedline.com
www.aladyexorcist.com

Table of Contents

The Spiritual (Spirit) Importance Of
Jesus' Call to Ministry

"The Spirit of the Lord is upon me because "He" hath anointed me to Preach the gospel to the poor: He hath sent me to Heal the Brokenhearted, to Preach Deliverance to the captives, and Recovering of sight to the Blind, To set at Liberty them that are Bruised" Luke 4:18. "And Jesus went about all Galilee teaching in their synagogues, and preaching the gospel of the kingdom and healing all manner of sickness."(Greek, Nosoinseo) to have a diseased appetite, to hanker after, (crave a sickness), dote upon, a malady, disability, infirmity, disease; clutching to self-an evil thing)...And all manner of disease... (Greek, Malakian, softness or weakness to disease)...among the people. And his fame went throughout all Syria and they brought unto "Him" all sick (frail, impotent) people that were taken with diverse diseases (held in the custody of, or is a prisoner of physical trouble), and torments..."Greek, Basnismos/Kakos-to, maltreatment, torture, make evil affected, vex, hurt, harm, pain, toil)...Those which were possessed with devils (Spirits) and those which were lunatic, and **HE HEALED THEM ALL.** Matthew 4:23-24 "Now when the sun was setting, all they that had any sick with divers diseases, brought them unto Him and He laid His hands on **EVERYONE OF THEM AND HEALED THEM, AND DEVILS (SPIRITS) ALSO CAME OUT OF MANY,** crying and saying "Thou Art Christ The Son of God, And He rebuked them suffering them not to speak; for they knew that He was Christ. Luke 4:40, Matthew 8:16, Now when Jesus was risen early the first day of the week He appeared first to Mary Magdalene, out of whom He had cast seven devils. (Spirits)" Mark 16:9" How God anointed Jesus of Nazareth with the Holy Ghost and with Power: who went about doing good and healing all that were oppressed of the devil (Spirits) for God was with him." Acts 10:38. "And Jesus knew their thoughts and said unto them, Every kingdom divided against itself is brought to desolation; and every city or house divided against itself shall not stand: And if Satan cast out Satan, he is divided against himself; how shall then his kingdom stand?…**But if I Cast Out Devils by, The Spirit of God, then The Kingdom of God is come unto you…He that is not with me is against me; and he that gathereth not with me scattereth abroad." Matt. 12:25-30. It is most interesting and vital to see how Our Lord and Savior Jesus Christ Ministered Salvation, Exorcism, Healing, Deliverance and Inner-Healing during "His" short walk on earth.** Notice that He healed all who came to "Him" of whatever problem, no matter how strong or violent the Spirits were. In some places where "He" ministered, people's faith was stronger and "He" could do more. This meant that although the Gift of healing within Jesus never changed or "Lost power" the faith level of those with whom Jesus worked with was subject to their, own allowed level of belief. In some places, The Son of God himself could not deliver or give healing because the people themselves were not ready to receive it. Hosea 4:6 says my people are destroyed for lack of knowledge. (The prophet was speaking here of the people of God.) Yet, Jesus Christ is the all-powerful Son of God, God himself and a strong deliverer in the day of trouble to those who turn to him. The Holy Spirit is the power for Deliverance there are about 1,700 places in The Word of God, denoting "Deliver" "Deliverance" and "Deliverer." And praise the Lord god, after a person has been delivered, set-free, liberated, healed and cleansed of evil spirits with all of their influence and control. (Spirits) The Kingdom of God which is Righteousness, Peace and Joy in The Holy Ghost, is the power that is endued upon them. "For the kingdom of God, is not meat and drink; but righteousness and peace and joy in The Holy Ghost. For he that in these things serveth Christ Is acceptable to God and approved of men. Romans 14:17-18. Jesus promised that his followers would do the same works that "He" did and even greater works than those that "He" did. The Believers, who hear "His" voice, believe "His Word" and become "His" disciples these two thousand years after the resurrection, continue to have this same promise and commission. "Verily, verily, I say unto you, he that believeth on me, the works that I do shall he do also; and greater works than these shall he do; because I go unto my Father. And whatsoever ye shall ask in my name, that will I do, that the Father may be glorified in the Son. If ye shall ask any thing in my name, I will do it. If ye love me keep my commandments." John 14:12-15 Jesus Christ, the same yesterday, and today and forever. Heb. 13:8 "And Jesus came and spake unto them saying **all power is given unto me in heaven and in earth. Go ye therefore, and teach all nations, baptizing them in the name of the Father, and of the Son, and of the Holy Ghost: Teaching them to observe all things whatsoever I have commanded you: and, Lo, I am with you always even unto the end of the world, Amen. Matt.28:18-20** "And He said unto them, Go ye into all the world, and preach the gospel to every creature. He that believeth and is baptized shall be saved; but them that believeth not shall be damned. And these signs shall follow them that believe; In my Name Shall they Cast Out Devils (Spirits); they shall speak with new tongues; They shall take up serpents (Spirits) and if they drink any deadly thing, It shall not hurt them; they shall lay hands on the sick, and they shall recover. Mark 16: 15-18 "And He (Jesus) said unto them, I beheld Satan as lightning fall from heaven. Behold, I give unto you power to tread on serpents (Spirits) and scorpions

(Spirits) and over all the power of the enemy (Jesus is speaking of the enemies Spiritual power here.) and nothing shall by any means hurt you. Not withstanding, in this rejoice not, that the Spirits are subject unto you; but rather rejoice, because your names are written in heaven. **In that hour Jesus rejoiced in Spirit, and said, I Thank thee, O Father, Lord of Heaven and Earth, that thou hast hid these things from the wise and prudent, and has revealed them unto babes: even so, Father, for it seemed good in they sight. Luke 10:18-21** But ye shall receive power (Spiritual Power) after that the Holy Ghost is come upon you: and "ye shall be witnesses unto…the uttermost part of the earth" Acts 1:8 **"Now The Spirit speaketh expressly (The Spirit of God) that in the latter times some shall depart from the faith giving heed to seducing spirits, and doctrines of devils."** The Word of God, The Bible pictures the last days as a period of time given over to the reign of demonic or evil spirits." 1 Tim 4:1. But God loves us and does not want us to perish and be lost forever. So he provided eternal life for us in the cross, death and resurrection of Jesus Christ who became our substitute and savior. Jesus bore our sins and our iniquities, and Jesus suffered for our transgressions. It is written that Jesus bore our pains, sicknesses, and infirmities: "Sure He has borne our griefs, sickness, weakness and distress…and carried our sorrows and pain (of punishment). Yet we ignorantly considered Him stricken, smitten and afflicted by God, But He (Jesus) was wounded for our transgressions, He (Jesus) was bruised for our guilt and iniquities; the chastisement (needful to obtain peace and well-being for us was upon Him (Jesus), and with the stripes that wounded Him we are Healed and made Whole. All we like sheep have gone astray, we have turned everyone to his own way; and the Lord has made to light on Him (Jesus) the guilt and iniquity of us all. Isaiah 53:4-6 (Amp. Bible) **For God so loved the world, that He gave his only begotten Son, that whosoever believeth in him should not perish, but have everlasting life. John 3:16. As many as received Him (Jesus), to them gave he power to become the sons of God. John 1:1 Jesus, said, "I am the way, the truth, and the life: no man cometh unto the Father, but by me, John 14:6 The Word of God says, He that hath the Son hath life, 1 John 5:12.** Jesus said, "**The Spirit** of the Lord is upon me, **because he hath anointed me to preach the gospel to the poor; he hath sent me to heal the brokenhearted, to preach deliverance to the captives, and recovering of sight to the blind; to set at liberty them that are bruised to preach the acceptable year of the Lord."** Luke 4:18, **Jesus said, this is why the Spirit of God had anointed "Him." That He might do something for the people who were hurting and in need. Jesus gave the Gospel to the poor. Jesus brought healing to the sick. Jesus announced, Deliverance to the captives, Jesus set at liberty those who were blind and bruised by life. Jesus told the people that the time God would accept them for Salvation, Healing and Deliverance was now.** Jesus is the same Yesterday, Today, Forever, and Jesus is saying, this promise is Good Right Now.

The Bible a Spirit Book, Written in a Spirit Language, To a Spirit People, From a Spirit God **"And we are setting these truths forth in words not taught by human wisdom but taught by the (Holy) Spirit. Combining and interpreting spirit truths with spirit language (to those who possess the Holy Spirit)** to the Spirit-Filled Believer, the spiritual realm relates to that which causes this natural world this "physical world of stuff" or physical (material) things to come alive, to move, to change or resist change, to take action (even when the action taken is deliberately not to take action). The Spiritual realm underlies all that happens in the natural or material world. **The natural or physical world is where the spiritual realm applies itself.** Thus, the two world or realms are different angles of the same reality operating within his world and within the lives of Spirit-Filled individuals. The world of God is full of references to the spiritual realm and our spirits but not very many Spirit-Filled Believers venture to discuss this very important issue that permeates all man kind. **The word of God says, "God can stir up the Spirit."** Haggai :14 "And the Lord stirred up the Spirit of Zerubbabel the son of Shealtiel, governor of Judah, and the spirit of Joshua the son of Josedech, the high priest, and the Spirit of all the remnant of the people; and they came and did work in the house of the lord of hosts, their God." **The word of God says, God searches the Spirit.** Proverbs 20:27 'The Spirit of man is the candle of the Lord, searching all the inward parts of the belly." **The word of God says, God gives us a new Spirit.** Ezekiel 36:26 "A new heart also will I give you, and a new Spirit will I put within you: and I will take away the stony heart out of your flesh, and I will give you a heart of flesh." **The word of God says that God gives our Spirit a New Birth,** John 3:6 "That which is born of the flesh is flesh; and that which is born of The Spirit is spirit." **The word of God tells us that, God testifies with our Spirit.** Romans 8:16 "The Spirit itself beareth witness with our Spirit, that we are the children of God."**The word of God says, our Spirit returns to "Him"** Ecclesiastes 12:7 "then shall the dust return to the earth as it was: and the Spirit shall return unto God who gave it." And then **the word of God says that God receives our Spirit.** Psalm 31:5 "Into thine hand I commit my Spirit: Thou hast redeemed me, O Lord God of truth." The spiritual realm extends to the heavens. John 4:24 says, **God is a Spirit** and they that worship "Him" must worship him in spirit and in truth." God is revealed in this world, as an infinite, Eternal. Self-existent Spirit who is the first Cause of all that is. Isaiah 66:1, says, "Thus saith the Lord, the heaven is my throne, and the earth is my footstool:" Jeremiah 23:24. Can any hide himself in secret places that I shall not see him? Saith the Lord. Do not I fill heaven and earth? Saith the Lord." Acts 17:24 "God that made the world and all things therein, seeing that he is Lord of Heaven and Earth, dwelleth not in temples made with hands." **God is eternal.** Psalms 90:2"Before the mountains were brought forth, or ever thou hadst formed the earth and the world, even from everlasting to everlasting, thou Art God." **God is holy.** Leviticus 11:44" For I Am the Lord your God: ye shall therefore sanctify yourselves, and ye shall be holy; for I am holy: neither shall; ye defile yourselves with any manner of creeping thing that creepeth upon the earth." **God is Immortal.** 1 Timothy 1:17 "Now unto the King eternal, immortal, invisible, the only wise God, be honor and glory forever and ever. Amen. **God is invisible** John 1:18 "No man hath seen God at any time; the only begotten Son, which is in the bosom of the Father, he hath declared him. **God is all powerful and incomparable." Isaiah 406-7; 18, 25** "the voice said, cry, and he said, what shall I cry? All flesh is grass, and all the goodliness thereof is as the flower of the field. The grass withereth, the flower fadeth: because the Spirit of the Lord bloweth upon it: surely the people is grass. To whom then will ye liken God? Or what likeness will ye compare unto him? To whom then will ye liken me, or shall I be equal? Saith the Holy One." **God is Righteous** Psalm 145:17 "The Lord is righteous in all his ways and Holy in all His works. **God is Unchanging** Malachi 3:6 says "For I am the Lord, I change not" **The Word of God says God is gracious and merciful.** Exodus 34:6 says "And the Lord passed by before him and proclaimed, The Lord, The Lord. God merciful and gracious, longsuffering and abundant in goodness and truth. Who is like unto thee, O Lord, among the gods? Who is like thee, glorious, in holiness, fearful in praises, doing wonders" **God is a Spirit (Invisible) meaning that God is not a physical being limited to one place. God is present everywhere and at the same time.** The word of God says, God created all things, "In heaven and in the earth" Gen. 1:1, in the beginning God created the heaven and the earth. Isaiah. 42:5 says, Thus saith God the Lord, he that created the heavens, and stretched them out: he that spread forth the earth, and that which cometh out of it; the that giveth breath unto the people upon it, and Spirit to them that walketh therein. Col. 1:16-17 says, "For by Him were all things created, that are in heaven and that are in earth, visible and invisible, whether they be thrones or dominions, or principalities, or powers: all things were created by Him and for Him. And He is before all things, and by Him all things consist. Here the Word of God affirms that by Christ Jesus, the eternal word of God were all things created, that are in heaven, visible in earth and invisible in the Spiritual realm. **Jesus Christ, the only begotten Son of God, preexistent with God, asserted in the Old Testament.** Isaiah 9:6 "For unto us a child is born, unto us a son is given: and the government shall be upon his shoulder: and his name shall be called Wonderful. Counselor, The mighty God, the everlasting Father, The Prince of Peace." **Jesus Christ Asserted in the New Testament. John 1:1 "In the beginning was the Word, and the Word was with God, and the Word was God." Col. 1:15 says, Who is the image of the invisible God, the firstborn of every creature. Rev. 1:8, " I am Alpha and Omega, the beginning and the ending, saith the Lord which is, and which was, and which is to come, the almighty.** Jesus equal and one with God, the Father. John 5:18 therefore the Jews sought the more to kill him, because he not only had broken the Sabbath, but said also that God was his Father, making himself equal with God. John 17:22. "And the glory which thou gavest me I have given them: that they may be one, even as we are one." **Jesus (God is a Spirit) the Word of God, became flesh and dwelt among us. Jesus shared our humanity, like us in all things except sin.** John 1:14, "And the word was made flesh, and dwelt among us, (and we beheld His glory, the glory as of the only begotten of the Father.0 full of grace and truth" Heb. 2:14 "For as much then as the children are partakers of flesh and blood, he also himself likewise took part of the same; that through death he might destroy him that had the power of death, that is the devil." Heb 4:15 "For we have not an high priest which cannot be touched with the feelings of our infirmities, but was in all points tempted like as we are, yet without sin." **Jesus, fulfilling Old Testament Prophecy and dying for our sins, reconciling us back to God and rising again for our justification, destroying the works of Satan,. Sending out the Holy Spirit and the Good News is that Jesus is coming again to take us to himself.** Luke 19:10"For the son of man is come to seek and to save that which was lost." **Jesus came to give us eternal life. John 10:10-30 "The thief cometh not, but for to steal, and to kill, and to destroy: I am come that they might have life, and that they might have it more abundantly. I am the good shepherd: the good shepherd giveth his life for the sheep.** But he that is a hireling, and not the shepherd, whose own the sheep are not, seeth the wolf coming and leaveth the sheep, and fleeth; and the wolf catcheth them, and scattereth the sheep. The hireling fleeth, because he is a hireling, and careth not for the sheep. I am the good shepherd, and know my sheep, and am known of mine. As the Father knoweth me, even so know I the Father: and I lay down my life for the sheep. And other sheep I have, which are not of this fold: them also I must bring and they shall hear my voice; and they shall be one fold, and one shepherd. Therefore doth my Father love me, because I lay down my life, that I might take it again. No man taketh it from, but I lay it down of myself. I have power to lay it down, and I have power to take it again. This commandment have I received of my Father. There was a division therefore again among the Jews for these saying. And many of them said, He hath a devil, and is mad; why hear ye him? Others said these are not the words of him that hath a devil; can a devil open the eyes of the blind? And it was at Jerusalem the feast of the dedication, and it was winter. And Jesus walked in the temple in Solomon's porch. Then came the Jews round about him, and said unto him. How long dost thou make us to doubt? If thou be the Christ, tell us plainly. Jesus answered them. I told you and ye believed not: the works that I do in my Father's name, they bear witness of me. But ye believed not; because ye are not of my sheep, as I said unto you. My sheep hear my voice, and I know them, and they follow me: And I give unto them eternal life; and they shall never perish, neither shall any man pluck them out of my hand. My Father, which gave them me, is greater than all; and no man is able to pluck them out of my Father's hand. I and my Father are one. Heb. 2:14-15" Forasmuch then as the children are partakers of flesh and blood, he also himself likewise took part of the same; that through death he might destroy him that had the power of death, that is the devil. And deliver them who through fear of death were all their lifetime subject to bondage." 1 John 3:8 says, "He that committeth sin is of the devil; for the devil sinneth from the beginning. For this purpose the Son of God was manifested, that he might destroy the works of the devil." **Jesus, rules the World and the Church today at God's** right hand. Eph 1:19-22 "And what is the exceeding greatness of his power to us-ward who believe, according to the working of his mighty power. Which he wrought in Christ, when he raised him from the dead, and set him at his own right hand in the heavenly places. Far above all principality, and power, and might, and dominion, and every name that is named, not only in this world, but also in that which is to come. And hath put all things under his feet, and gave him to be the head over all things to the church." Col. 1:18 says, "And he is the head of the body, the church: who is the beginning, the firstborn from the dead; that in all things he might have the preeminence. For it pleased the Father that in him should all fullness dwell; And having made peace through the blood of his cross, by him to reconcile all things unto himself; by him I say, whether they be things in earth, or things in heaven." **Jesus is The Word of God. Rev. 19: 11-13 says, "And I saw heaven opened, and behold a white horse; and he that sat upon him was called Faithful and true** and in righteousness he doth judge and make war. His eyes were as a flame of fire, and on his head were many crowns; and he had a name written, that no man knew, but he himself. And he was clothed with a vesture dipped in blood: and his name is called **The Word of God." And Jesus is Alive today, living within the Spirit of everyone that has asked him to come in and become their Lord and Savior.** Rev. 1:18 says, "I am he that liveth, and was dead; and behold, I am alive forever more, Amen; and have keys of hell and of death." And when the day of Pentecost was fully come, they were all with one accord in one place. And suddenly there came a sound from heaven as of a rushing mighty wind, and it filled all the house where they were sitting. And there appeared unto them cloven tongues like as of fire, and it sat upon each of them, and they were all filled with The Holy Ghost, (Holy Spirit) and began to speak with other tongues, as the Spirit gave them utterance." The Holy Spirit, like the Father and the Son, a divine person of the Godhead. The Holy Spirit is eternal. Everywhere present, almighty, perfect, wise, perfectly just, as the Father is the creator, and the Son is the Savior and Redeemer, The Holy Spirit is the Sanctifier who frees us to lead new lives. **The Holy Spirit comes and Indwells us, The Spirit of God, The Spirit of Jesus, The Holy Spirit comes to live within us** causing our human spirit to become regenerated or born-again, born of God. John 14: 16-17 "And I will pray the Father, and He shall give you another comforter, that he may abide with you forever; even the Spirit of truth; whom the world cannot receive, because it seeth him not, neither knoweth him: but ye know him; For he dwelleth with you, and shall be in you." Rom. 8:11: "But if the Spirit of him that raised up Jesus from the dead dwell in you, he that raised up Christ from the dead shall also quicken your mortal bodies by "His Spirit" that dwelleth in you." Once the Holy Spirit comes and lives within us, He begins the wonderful work of changing us to become conformed to the likeness of our Lord and Savior Jesus Christ; **The Holy Spirit convicts us of our sins.** John 16: 7-11 "Nevertheless I tell you the truth, it is expedient for you that I go away: For if I go not away, the Comforter will not come unto you; but if I depart, I will send him unto you. And when he is come, he will reprove the world of sin, and of righteousness, and of judgment: Of sin, because they believe not one me; of righteousness, because I go to my Father, and ye see me no more; of judgment because the prince of this world is judged." **The Holy Spirit gives us a New Life.** John 3:5-7"Jesus answered, Verily, verily, I say unto thee, except a man be born of water, and of the Spirit, he cannot enter into the Kingdom of God. That which is born of the flesh is flesh and that which is born of the Spirit is Spirit. Marvel not that I said unto thee, **ye must be Born-Again.** Titus 3:5 "Not by works of righteousness which we have done, but according to his mercy he saved us, by the washing of regeneration, and renewing of The Holy Ghost. Which he shed on us abundantly through Jesus Christ our Savior." **The Holy Spirit Prays for Us in Times of Crisis.** Rom 8:26-27 "Likewise the Spirit also helpeth our infirmities for we know not what we should pray for as we ought: but the Spirit itself maketh intercession for the saints according to the Will of God." **The Holy Spirit enables us to find and know the truth of God.** 1 John 4:1-6 "Beloved, believe not every spirit, but try the spirits whether they are of god: because many false prophets are gone out into the world, hereby know ye the Spirit of God: Every spirit that confesseth that Jesus Christ is come in the flesh is of God: And every spirit that confesseth not that Jesus Christ is come in the flesh is not of God: and this is that Spirit of antichrist, whereof ye have heard that is should come: and even now already is it in the world. Ye are of God, little children, and have overcome them: because greater is he that is you, than he that is in the world. They are of the world: therefore speak they of the world, and the world heareth them. We are of God: he that knoweth God heareth us; he that is not of God heareth not us. Hereby know we the Spirit of truth, and the spirit of error. **The Holy Spirit makes us realize God's Love.** Rom. 5:5 "And hope maketh not ashamed; because the love of God is shed abroad in our hearts by The Holy Ghost which is given unto us. " **The Holy Spirit keeps us in Touch with God.** Rom. 8: 26-27 "Likewise the Spirit also helpeth our infirmities; for we now not what we should pray for as we ought: but the Spirit itself maketh intercession for us with groanings which cannot be uttered. And he that searcheth the hearts knoweth what is the mind of the Spirit, because he maketh intercession for the saints according to the will of God." Jude 20: "But ye, beloved, building up yourselves on your most holy faith, praying in the Holy Ghost." **The Holy Spirit enables us to live the Victorious, Spirit-filled life.** Rom. 8:5-11 "For they that are after the flesh do mind the things of the flesh; but they that are after the Spirit, the things of the spirit. For to be carnally minded is death: but to be spiritually minded is life and peace. Because the carnal mind is enmity against God: for it is not subject to the law of God, neither indeed can be. So then they that are in the flesh cannot please God. But ye are not in the flesh, but in the Spirit, if so be that the Spirit of God dwell in you. Now if any man have not the Spirit of Christ, he is none of his. And if Christ be in you, the body is dead because of sin; but the Spirit is life because of righteousness. But if the Spirit of him that raised up Jesus from the dead dwell in you, he that raised up Christ from the dead shall also quicken you mortal bodies by his Spirit that dwelleth in you. **"The Holy Spirit gives to us the Joy and the Peace of God.** Rom. 14:17 "For the Kingdom of God is not meat and drink; but Righteousness and peace, and Joy in The Holy Ghost." **The Holy Spirit gives us Power to be a witness for God.** "But ye shall receive power, after that The Holy Ghost is come upon you: and ye shall be witnesses unto me both in Jerusalem, and in all Judea, and in Samaria, and unto the uttermost part of the earth." **The Holy Spirit brings the presence of Jesus to us.** John 14: 16-18 "And I will pray the Father, and he shall give you another comforter, that he may abide with you forever; Even the Spirit of truth; whom the world cannot receive, because it seeth him not, neither knoweth him: but ye know him: for he dwelleth with you, and shall be in you. I will not leave you comfortless: I will come to you." **The Holy Spirit works "His" fruit within us.** Gal. 5:16-25."This I say then, walk in the Spirit, and ye shall not fulfill the lust of the flesh. For the flesh lusteth against the Spirit, and the Spirit against the flesh: and these are contrary the one to the other; so that ye cannot do the things that ye would. But if ye be led of the Spirit, ye are not under the law. Now the works of the flesh are manifest, which are these, adultery, fornication, uncleanness, lasciviousness, Idolatry, witchcraft, hatred, variance, emulations, wrath, strife, seditions, heresies, envyings, murders, drunkenness, revelings, and such like. Of the which I tell you before, as I have also told you in time past that they which do such things shall not inherit the Kingdom of God. **"But the fruit of the Spirit is Love, Joy, Peace, Long-suffering, Gentleness, Goodness, Faith, Meekness, Temperance:** against such there is no law. And they that are Christ's have crucified the flesh with the affections and lusts. If we live in the Spirit, let us also walk in the Spirit." **The Holy Spirit gives us gifts.** 1 Cor.12: 4-11 "Now there are diversities of gifts, but the same Spirit. And there are differences of administrations, but the same Lord. And there are diversities of operations, but it is the same God which worketh all in all. But the manifestations of the Spirit is given to every man to profit withal. One is given the Word of wisdom; to another the Word of Knowledge, by the same Spirit; to another Faith by the same Spirit; to another the gifts of Healing by the same Spirit; to another the working of Miracles; to another Prophecy; to another Discerning of Spirits; to another Diver Kinds of Tongues; to another the Interpretation of Tongues. But all these worketh that one and the selfsame Spirit, dividing to every man severally as he wills. **God, One God in Three Equal Spiritual Persons and Spiritual Operation, God, The Father, the creator of everything, God the Son, Redeemer, Lord and Savior, God the Holy Spirit, sanctifying, Power of God. "Unto thee it was shown, that thou mightest know that the Lord he is God; there is none else beside Him."** According to the Word of God Jesus was equipped for His earthly ministry by, being baptized in the Jordan River by, John the Baptist. Matthew 3:16 And Jesus, when He was baptized, went up straightway out of the water: and, lo, **the heavens were opened unto him and he saw the Spirit of God descending** like a dove and lighting upon him. The Bible then tells us in Matthew 4: 1, that the Holy Spirit led Jesus to the wilderness, it reads "then was Jesus led up of the Spirit, (The Holy Spirit) into the wilderness to be tempted of the devil. Jesus, then **being fully man and supernaturally indwelt by the Holy Spirit, was able to face Satan, a supernatural evil spirit, who is indwelt by the personification and manifestation of all that is evil. Jesus was able to resist all of his temptations. Jesus began his earthly ministry by preaching to the people** "Repent: for the kingdom of God is at hand." Jesus began his ministry in the Synagogue or the Church by ministering, (reading) out to the Word of God. "The Spirit of the Lord is upon me, because he hath anointed me to preach the gospel to the poor**; he hath sent me to heal the broken-hearted, to preach deliverance to the captives, and recovering of sight to the blind, to set at liberty them that are bruised. To preach the acceptable year of the Lord.** Luke 4:18. Then Jesus began to operate in His ministry, spiritually having been endued with power from on high, from our Father God. **Power that had been given to Him supernaturally from the Holy Spirit. Power that enabled Jesus to turn water into wine. Power that enabled Jesus to heal an official's son at Capernaum. Power that enabled Jesus to cast-out-a- demon in Capernaum. Power that enabled Jesus to heal Peter's Mother-in-law. Supernatural power endued to Jesus from the Holy Spirit that enabled Jesus to heal a leper, cause some frustrated fishermen to catch a haul of fish, heal a paralytic, heal a crippled man, heal a man's hand that had shriveled up, heal a centurion's servant, raise a widow's son from the dead, sill a storm, heal a woman's bleeding, raise Jairus' daughter from the dead, heal two blind men, heal a mute man, feed five thousand people, walk on water, feed another four thousand, heal a deaf man, cast demons out of a boy, provide a temple tax for Peter and himself from a fish's mouth, heal ten lepers, heal a man from dropsy, speak a word a fig tree died, speak another word and Lazarus was raised from the dead.** Jesus did all of this while He was alive here on this earth through the supernatural power "He" received when he was supernaturally endued with power from on high by The Holy Spirit. **Then the Bible goes on to say that Jesus died and was resurrected, through that same supernatural power of God, the Holy Spirit.** The Word of God says that God created two classes of Spiritual beings in heaven. Good and Evil. The good spiritual beings described as Man, Seraphim, cherubim and Angels. And the evil spiritual beings described as Principalities, Powers, Rulers of darkness and Wicked Spirits Eph 6:12. Thrones, Dominions, Col 1:16 Fallen Angels, 2 Peter 2:4 Spirits in Prison, 1 Peter 3:18-20 Seducing Spirits, Devils, 1 Tim. 4:1 Spirit of Jealousy Num 5:14, Familiar Spirits 1 Sam 28:7, Spirit of Deep Sleep Isaiah. 29:10 Spirit of Whoredoms, Hosea. 4:12, Unclean Spirits, Luke 8:29, Spirits of Infirmity Luke 13:11, Spirit of Divination Acts 16:16, Spirit of Bondage Rom. 8:15, Enticing Spirit 2 Chronicles. 18:20, Spirit of Devils, Rev. 16:14, Spirits of False Prophets 1John 4:1 Seducing Spirits 1Tim 4:1, Angel of light, disguised as 2 Corinthians. 1:14, The Tormentors Matt 18:34, Spirit of Fear 2 Tim 1:7, Spirit of Antichrist 1 John 4:3, Spirit of Error 1 John 4:6, Foul Spirit, Rev. 18:2, Another Spirit 2 Cor. 11:4, Spirit of the World 1 Cor 2:12, Spirit of Heaviness, Isaiah. 61:3, Perverse Sprit, Isaiah. 19:14, Lying Spirit 2 Chron. 18:22, Prideful Spirit Prov. 16:18, and other Spirits, (study your Bible) Satan, Lucifer. The Anointed Cherub, Isaiah. 14: 12-17. Ezek

28:12-19 and Demons. The word of God says that Seraphim have three pairs of wings, and we know that there are at least four of them, though there could be more. The Seraphim attend the Lord's throne, and call attention to "His" holiness. They are referred to as the four beasts, or living creatures, around the throne of God. They each have a different face. The first, the face of a man, the second, the face of a calf, the third the face of a flying eagle. The fourth, the face of a lion, they have eyes in front and behind them. Rev.4:6-8. The Cherubim have only two pairs of wings, but each has four faces. The face in front is that of a man; the right side that of a lion; the left side that of an Ox (calf) and the back that of an eagle. They also have the hand of a man under their wings on each of the four sides. Ezek.1:4-25; 10:1-22. Then the Word of God speaks of Angels, saying that they are innumerable in number, in Heb. 12:22. The Word of God says that they are mighty in power, and excel in strength. One Angel wiped out 185,000 troops of the Assyrian Army in one night. 2Kings 19:35, The Word of God says that Angels are Ministering Spirits to them that are the heirs of salvation. Heb. 1:13, 14, The Word of God says, that God's Angels are the executioners of God's wrath on the wicked. 2 Thess.1:7, 8, The Word of God says that God's Angel's will gather the elect of Israel from the four corners of the earth. Matt. 24:31 and The Word of God says that God's Angels are commissioned to supply the needs of God's people in, Matt. 4:11, and 1 Kings 19:4-8. In the Word of God there are three prominent Angels of God that are known by name, one is Michael, also called an Arch-angel. Another is Gabriel and then we have Lucifer, a.k.a, Satan.

The Word of God has much to say concerning Satan. Ezek. 28:14-19, tells us that the Angel (Spiritual being) Satan" Thou art the anointed cherub that covereth; and I have set thee so: thou wast upon the holy mountain of God; thou hast walked up and down in the midst of the stones of fire. Thou wast perfect in thy ways from the day that thou was created, till iniquity was found in thee. By the multitude of they merchandise they have filled the midst of thee with violence, and thou has sinned: therefore I will cast thee as profane out of the mountain of God: and I will destroy thee, O covering cherub, from the midst of the stones of fire. Thine heart was lifted because of thy beauty; thou has corrupted thy wisdom by reason of thy brightness: I will cast thee to the ground; I will lay thee before Kings, that they may behold thee. Thou hast defiled thy sanctuaries by the multitude of thine iniquities, by the iniquity of thy traffic; therefore will I bring forth a fire from the midst of thee, it shall devour thee, and I will bring thee to ashes upon the earth in the sight of all them that behold thee. All they that know thee among the people shall be astonished at thee: thou shalt be a terror, and never shalt thou be any more. Let's take a close look at these scriptures; First Satan was a created (Spirit) being, created by God as a Spirit being an angel. Second, he was perfect in his original creation. Third he was the anointed Cherub. The word cherub in scripture always denotes "a spirit being" that is in close relationship to God. Fourth he was appointed by God to hold an exalted position. Fifth, he sinned against God. The account of Satan's fall is also recorded in Isaiah. 14:12-17, it says "how art thou fallen from heaven, O Lucifer, son of the morning" How art thou cut down to the ground, which didst weaken the nations! For thou has said. In thine heart, I will ascend into heaven, I will exalt my throne above the stars of God: I will sit also upon the mount of the congregation, in the sides of the north: I will ascend above the heights of the clouds; I will be like the most High. Yet thou shalt be brought down to hell, to the sides of the pit. They that see thee shall narrowly look upon thee, and consider thee saying, is this the man that made the earth to tremble, that did shake kingdoms; that made the world as a wilderness, and destroyed the cities thereof; that opened not the house of his prisoners. Satan led a revolt of Angels **(Spirit Beings)** in heaven and successfully tempted Eve and Adam in the Garden of Eden to sin against the Authority of God's Word. The Angel Spirit, Lucifer, is the leader of the kingdom of Evil. Jesus said in Luke 10:18 "And he said unto them, I beheld Satan as lightning fall from heaven." Rev. 12:7-9 "And there was war in heaven: Michael and his angels (good spirits) fought against the dragon: And the dragon fought and his angels, (evil spirits) and prevailed not; neither was their place found any more in heaven. And the great dragon was cast out, that old Serpent, called the Devil and Satan, which deceiveth the whole world: he was cast out into the earth, and his angels were cast out with him. I believe that those fallen angels that were cast out of heaven with Lucifer are what we now call Demons, Evil Spirits, Unclean Spirits and many other names. God created nothing in its origin that was evil. Lucifer, who later became the devil, was created perfect by God before his fall. Therefore other spiritual beings (Angels) must also have been created perfect before their fall under the leadership of Lucifer and became demons, (evil spirits. The Spirit-filled believer faces a spiritual conflict with demons and a host of other evil spirits, these spiritual forces constitute, the powers of darkness with Satan being the god of this world system. The Devil energizes the ungodly, and opposes the Will of God upon this earthly realm. Satan and his hosts constitute a vast multitude, and they are organized into a highly systematized spiritual empire of evil with rank and order. All who are without Jesus Christ are controlled by "The prince of the power of the air" Satan and their minds are blinded by him to the truth of God. They are enslaved to sin, the lusts of the flesh and by these hosts of evil spirits. These evil spirits are wicked, unclean, vicious, and have the power to derange both mind and body. They have the ability to cause Dumbness, Blindness, Insanity, Suicidal Mania, Personal injuries, Inflicting physical defect and deformities. Make no mistake about it Satan's power is limited by God. However at the same time you must realize that His spiritual power is very real. He beguiled Eve, 2Cor.11:3, He uses magical and psychic power. Ex. 7:11-12, He empowered a witch to bring forth a spirit 1Sam. 28:12-20, He is called the god of forces Dan. 11:13, He wars against the Angels of God, Dan. 10:13, If these Spirit beings are so real, some might ask, why can't we see them? Ask yourself this question how many people believe that a glass of water is full of little wiggling bits of life? Of course, we all believe it. That water is full of germ life, and if we could look at a drop through the microscope right now, it would come alive with movement. There are lots of things that are real that we cannot see with out natural eyes or hear with our natural ears. The room where you are sitting or standing right now is full of voices of all kinds. Music is filling the room at this very moment, but you can't hear it. But all you need to do is bring in a radio and turn it on, immediately then we can hear these sounds which fill the air. Another way that I can describe this Spiritual realm that the Bible assures us that it exists is something like a virtual reality in which a Spiritual version of our lives is being lived out (only it is within us) simultaneously with our natural lives. The Spiritual realm is an unseen realm, with the dividing line or veil between the natural realm and the Spiritual realm being our bodies. You and I have a body, but we are Spirits and we have a Soul, our Spirit dwells within our bodies. We express ourselves with the faculties of our bodies. We can see our bodies, but we cannot see our real selves, because or real self is a Spirit living inside or (within) our bodies. Our body is simply the temporary house that our Spirits live within. Someday our bodies will die and return to the dust, but our Spirit and our Soul shall never die. We shall return to God where we came from. Our Bodies are the instruments through which our Spirit and Soul expresses itself, cut our tongues out and our spirit could not talk. Destroy our ears and we could not hear, blind our eyes and we could not see, even though our eyes would be blind our ears deaf and our tongues removed, our Spirits, would still be there, but unable to see, hear, or speak. Amputate our legs and arms, destroy our sense of smell and our vocal cords, and still you could not have destroyed our Spirit or our Soul. However; our Spirit and Soul could no longer express it self. Our Spirit and Soul would still have a body, but its faculties of expression would have been destroyed. Our human bodies have the broadest means of expression, having been the only creation made in the image and likeness of God. Gen. 1:26, "And God said, let us make man in our image, after our likeness and let them have dominion over the fish of the sea, and over the foul of the air, and over the cattle, and over all the earth, and over every creeping thing that creepeth upon the earth. So God created man in his own image, in the image of God created he him; male and female created he them. "Gen. 2:7,"And the Lord God formed man of the dust of the ground, and breathed into his nostrils the breath of life; and man became a living soul." (A living Soul, Spirit, Human Being)** Evil Spirits seek as their highest prize to enter into a human being through which they can find expression. Since Evil Spirits, or Demons are actually spirit beings they can manifest their own personalities in the persons whom they are influencing or inhabiting, and they delight to use people to do their dirty work. God uses human instruments to minister to the human family; likewise, Satan uses human instruments to defile and to abuse the human family in his attempt to destroy God's most prized possession…One thing is certain Evil Spirits cannot rest without being in possession of some-body (**Fleshly Body**) through which they can find expression. **The Bible clearly explains to us that the Spiritual realm within us is as real as the natural realm without and about us. In fact the Spiritual realm determines what takes place in the natural realm.** The Word of God informs us that there are three heavens. 2 Cor. 12:2 says the first heaven is the atmosphere above the earth, the second heaven is the starry constellation or stellar heaven and the Third heaven is the abode of God. Although the location of heaven is up high above the earth, its operation is all over the earth and within us at the same time within our Spirits. Once you and I received the Lord Jesus Christ, as our Lord and Savior, Jesus came to live in our hearts, (Which was also a spiritual experience)

At that point we gained access to the heavenly or spiritual realm through Jesus Christ. Col. 1:27. To whom God would make known what is the riches of the glory of this mystery among the Gentiles: which is Christ in you, the hope of glory. The Spiritual realm or the Heavenly realm is where god has "His" provision for us. To receive from the Spiritual realm or the

Heavenly realm is where God has "His" provision for us. To receive from the Spiritual or Heavenly realm and bring it into our natural realm. Our Salvation is a beautiful example. We receive the salvation of Jesus Christ by faith and become Children of God John 1:12-13"But as many as received "Him" to them gave he power to become the Sons of God John 1:12-13 "But as many as received "Him" to them gave he power to become the Sons of God, even to them that believe on his name. Which were born, not of blood, nor of the will of the flesh, nor of the will of man, but of God. Our faith reached out to take something that already existed in the Spiritual or Heavenly realm. **Jesus has already died for us, that is true. But except a person reaches out by faith and receives Jesus into his or her heart the Salvation of Jesus (although invisible to the natural eye) already available spiritually will not benefit that person. "The Spiritual or Heavenly realm is a very real world, invisible to the natural eye but visible to and through the eyes of faith." Being born naturally puts you in your natural family and being Born-Again of the Spirit of God puts you in the family of God. Thus being Spirit Alive.** God promised that when the life and power of "His" Spirit would come upon "His" people, that they would be enabled to prophesy, see visions, have prophetic dreams, live a life of obedience, holiness and righteousness and witness with great power and authority. Joel 2:28-29 says "And it shall come to pass afterward, that I will pour out my Spirit upon all flesh; and your Sons and your Daughters shall prophesy, your old men shall dream dreams, your young men shall see visions. And also upon the servants and upon the hand maids in those days will I pour out my Spirit. **The Spirit realm exists and is made up of God, and a whole and complete realm of Spirit existence, with God, being ruler over everything Natural and Spirit.**

You Are a Spirit Sent From God, To Affect this Earth, Before Your Spirit Returns to God A Spirit Who Sent You Jesus ascended into heaven and sat down at the right hand of His Father and Our Father as co-ruler of God's Kingdom. In this exalted position Jesus having received the power of The Holy Spirit sent The Holy Spirit forth upon His people at Pentecost. **This out pouring testifies to the continual presence and the authority of Jesus this day.** The Holy Spirit came to this earth to indwell within Believers, filling them with God's supernatural power from on high through "His Spirit" just like He had filled "His Son Jesus" And when the day of Pentecost was fully come; they were all with one accord in one place. And suddenly there came a sound from heaven as of a rushing mighty wind, and it filled all the house where they were sitting. And there appeared unto them cloven tongues like as of fire, and it sat upon each of them. **And they were all filled with the Holy Ghost (Filled with the Holy Spirit, the beginning of a spiritual or supernatural experience with Jesus took place at that moment) and began to speak with other tongues, as The Spirit (The Holy Spirit, endued them with the second natural part of that supernatural experience with the third person of the Trinity) gave them utterance.** They had been filled with the Spirit of God and the Spirit of God supernaturally gave them a new language in order that they could communicate in the Kingdom of God. So the Holy Spirit came and the Church of Jesus Christ was born on earth that day. The day the power of God was manifested on earth, the supernatural power of God. Today **the Holy Spirit is now present in everyone who has asked "Him" to come and indwell them, trusting Jesus Christ as Savior and Lord.** Because the Holy Spirit is indwelling every Spirit-Filled Believer, you have immediately become a spiritual human being having been born-again baptized into the Spiritual Kingdom of God again. You see the Bible says in Genesis 1: In the beginning God created…Genesis 1:26 And God said, "Let us make man in our image, after our likeness and let them have dominion over the fish of the sea and over the fowl of the air, and over the cattle, and over all the earth, and over every creeping thing that creepeth upon the earth. Genesis 1:27, so God created man in his own image, in the image of God created he them" **"And God blessed them…be fruitful and multiply, and replenish the earth, and subdue it…and have**

dominion…over every living thing that moveth upon the earth. Genesis 1:31 and God saw everything that he had made, and behold, it was very good. Genesis 2:7 And the Lord God formed man of the dust of the ground and breathed into his nostrils the breath of life and man became a living soul. Ecclesiastes 12:6, 7 or ever the silver cord be loosed, or the golden bowl be broken, or the pitcher be broken at the fountain or the wheel broken at the cistern. Then shall the dust return to the earth as it was: **And the Spirit shall return unto God who gave it.** Do you know who you are? You are a Spirit sent from God, pause and think about that for a moment, say out loud **I am a spirit sent from God, to affect this earth before I return to God who sent me! If you are born-again and Holy Spirit filled your inner spirit man just registered the entire truth of that statement.** You see when you were a child; you knew exactly who you were, because you had just recently come from God. It took the world, Lust of the eye, Lust of the flesh and the Pride of Life, many years to train you to forget who you really are. To train you to believe that you are what they the world and the devil says that you are. Every living human being is a spirit sent from God whether they know it or not, the question is has their Human Spirit, been born-again, Re-born of the Spirit of God. You see when you as a Born-again Spirit-Filled Believer begin to understand and acknowledge that about yourself, you will also begin to understand and acknowledge it about others also. When you are able to believe and understand that: **You are a Spirit sent from God and that you, yes, you are made in the image and likeness of God.** You will begin like never before to recognize, appreciate and love that same Spirit of God in other Spiritual human beings, especially Holy Spirit-Filled Believers because they are also, filled with the same Holy Spirit, God that you are. Once you get this revelation and come to this understanding you will begin to have a depth of spiritual understanding and you will begin to operate through your spiritual understanding. Right now, today let's dispel the misunderstanding; let's get rid of any spiritual ignorance, doubt and unbelief, so that you can mature spiritually. You and I are **Spirits that live in a fleshly body; we have been sent from God Our Father. You and I are made in the image and likeness of Jesus Our Brother, Father, Savior and Lord. Made in Our Father God's Image and likeness. The Bible says that God is a Spirit and the Bible says that God's Spirit is within you! You cannot connect with God to receive anything from God, outside of your Spiritual self!** God's power is within you, God's very nature and character is within you all that God is, operating within you. God is a part of you within you operating from within you on the inside of you and working on the outside of you. God is a part of you operating from the outside of you to the inside of you! Think about that, Almighty God, you are a part of God from the inside out and you are a part of God from the outside in (Its all supernatural) **You became a Spiritual Supernatural part of God, through His Son Jesus, by the reuniting power of the cross at Calvary, by the shed blood of Jesus that purchased your Salvation and by the Baptism of God's Holy Spirit. You have been spiritually immersed into God, filled with Our Father God, Jesus, by "His" Holy Spirit. You were a Spirit sent from God originally and you became a re-united spirit with your creator, re-born, of the Spirit of God what you First were you have become again.** Now a Spiritual Part of God, A soul living spirit part of God, A part of God, A flesh submitted, Spirit of God dominated by God, ruled and led by God. A part of God, all of God is invested in you and God desires that you have understanding, wisdom and knowledge of "Him" his part of you, within you through "His Spirit" by His will in operation through His Spirit within you here on earth. **You are a Spirit of God, sent from God, to affect this earth so, God communicates to you Spiritually by "His" Spirit to "His" Spirit man by way of "His Holy Spirit" within "His Spirit Person you.** This is what is referred to as being led by The Spirit of God. This is also what is meant by Living in the Spirit. For as many as are led by the Spirit of God, they are the Sons of God. Entitled to have and maintain an intimate Loving relationship with God, The Father, Jesus, The Son and God the Holy Spirit. Due to our Spiritual relationship with God, We are called to surrender ourselves to the leading of the Holy Spirit and to the Lordship of Jesus Christ. As we make this surrender. The Power of the Holy Spirit is released within us, spiritually, supernaturally transforming us from within. I really want to emphasis this point: **Genesis 1: In the beginning God created…Genesis 1:26 and God said**, *Let us make man in our image, after our likeness and let them have dominion over the fish of the sea and over the fowl of the air, and over the cattle, and over all the earth, and over every creeping thing that creepeth upon the earth."* **Genesis 1:27** So God created man in his own Image, in the image of God created he them, And God blessed them…be fruitful and multiply, and replenish the earth, and subdue it…and have dominion…over every living thing that moveth upon the earth. **Genesis 1:31**And God saw everything that he had made, and behold, it was very good. **Genesis 2:7** And the Lord God formed man of the dust of the ground and breathed into his nostrils the breath of life and man became a living soul. **Ecclesiastes 12:6-7**, or ever the silver cord be loosed, or the golden bowl be broken, or the pitcher be broken at the fountain or the wheel broken at the cistern. Then shall the dust return to the earth as it was: **And the Spirit (You) shall return unto God who gave it.** You Are A Spirit Sent From God. "Pause, think about that for a moment" You Are a Spirit sent from God to Affect

this Earth! # Say this out loud

I_____Am a Spirit,
(Insert your name here)

Sent from God. To affect This Earth for God before my Spirit returns to God, Who sent it here, according to "His" plan and purpose. If you are Born-Again and Holy Spirit-Filled Your Inner-Spiritual Man just registered **The entire truth of that statement.** You see when you were a child; you knew exactly who you were, because you had just come from God. Just like the baby Jesus' spirit had, when Mary gave birth to our Savior. It took the world, *Lust of the eye, Lust of the flesh and The Pride of life,* many years to train you to forget who you are. To Train you to believe that you are, what they the World and the Devil says that you are. Every Living Human being is a Spirit sent From God, whether you or they know it or not. When you as a Born-again Spirit Filled, Believer begin to understand and acknowledge that about yourself, you will also begin to understand and acknowledge it about others. When you are able to believe and understand that: You are a Spirit sent from God and that, you, **yes; you** are made in the image and likeness of God. You will begin like never before to recognize, appreciate and Love that same Spirit of God in Other Spirit human beings.

Especially Holy Spirit-Filled Believers. Because they are also, Filled with the same Holy Spirit, God that you are. Once you come to this understanding you will begin to have a depth of Spiritual Understanding and you will begin to operate through your spiritual understanding. Right Now, today let's dispel the misunderstanding today let's get rid of any Spiritual Ignorance Doubt and Unbelief, so that you can mature spiritually. You and I Are Spirits sent from God. You and I are made in the image and likeness of Jesus. Made in God's Image and Likeness, God Is a Spirit! God's Spirit Is Within You! You cannot connect with God to receive anything from God outside of your Spiritual self! All of God's power is within you, All that God Is, Is Within You, God is a part of You, Within You operating from within on the Inside of You to the outside of You and God is a part of you operating from the outside of You to the inside of You! Almighty God!

You are a part of God from, the Inside Out and You are a part of God from the Outside In. You became your Re-connected part of God through Jesus by the Re-Uniting Power of God through Salvation and
By The Baptism of God's Holy Spirit.

We Were Spirit Immersed back into God our Father, Filled with Our Father God, by "His" Holy Spirit. You, Yes you, were a Spirit sent from God, You become a Re-United, Re-born, Spirit, Re-born of the Spirit of God what you first were you have become once again. Now a Spirit part of God a Soul living Spirit part of God, a part of God, a Flesh submitted, Spirit of God, that is supposed to be dominated by God through, "His" Holy Spirit, ruled and led by God a part of God. All of God is invested in you! And God desires that you have Understanding, Wisdom and Knowledge of "Him" His Part of you, that is living resident within you through "His Spirit" according to "His" will, plan and purpose, In operation through "His Spirit" within you here on this Earth, You are a Spirit of God, sent from God, to affect this earth so, God communicates to you spiritually by His Spirit to His Spirit by way of "HIS" Holy Spirit. Within "His" Spirit person you, this is what is referred to as born of the Spirit of God, thus being able to be led By the Spirit. Of God that is living and alive within YOU. This is also what is meant by, for as many as are led by The Spirit of God, They Are the Sons of God! This should also help you to understand why you have to wage a Spiritual Warfare! Through your spirit by, prayer, because your Father's enemy now has become your mortal enemy. **Satan, Evil, the devil, Invisible to the Natural eye. Is a Spirit. His Demons, Fallen Angels, Demonic Influence, Evil, Unclean, Infirmity, Spirits of Bondage, are also invisible to the natural eye and they are Spirits.** Just like your Spirit is Invisible to the natural eye. Just like God is a Spirit, invisible to the natural eye, but made visible to and through your

Spiritual Eyes. And they that Worship "HIM" God Spirit must Worship "HIM" In Spirit and In Truth. Invisible to the natural eye, but realized and known through your Spirit and Spiritual Eyes understood and realized through the eyes of your Spiritual Understanding. **You are a Spirit that lives in a body that has a Soul, sent from God to affect this earth.** The Apostle Paul prayed for you and me. That the eyes of our understanding be (are) enlightened, that we may know what is The Hope of Our Calling, and what the riches of The Glory of Our Inheritance Is in the Saints. We Are spirits sent, Called and Chosen, sent by God. To affect this earth. Ushering In the Kingdom Of God. Ephesians 1:3 Blessed be the God and Father of our Lord Jesus Christ, who hath blessed us with all Spiritual Blessings in Heavenly places **In Christ Jesus.** Now you know who you are, now you know why you were born. Now you know what you were sent here to do by God and for God. Before our Spirit returns to God, who sent it Now I want you to understand just how easy it is to Connect and Receive from Your Father God. **Matthew 18:19, 20, If two of you shall agree on earth as touching anything that they shall ask it shall be done for them of my Father which is in heaven. For where two or three are gathered together in my name, there Am I in the midst of them. "I am in the midst of them, Jesus"** and in that day ye shall ask me nothing, Verily, Verily, I say unto you, whatsoever ye shall ask the Father in My Name, he will give it you. Hitherto have ye asked me nothing In My Name: Ask, and Ye shall Receive, that your joy may be full. John 16: 23,24, "Jesus, **This is the confidence that we have"** 1John 5:13,14,15, These things have I written unto you that believe on the Name of The Son of God; that you may know that ye have eternal life, and that ye may believe on the Name of the Son of God. And this is the confidence that we have in him, that if we ask any thing according to his will, he heareth us; and if we know that he hear us whatsoever we ask, we know that we have the petitions that we desired of him. **Again I say unto you, that if two of you shall agree on earth as touching anything that they shall ask, It shall be done for them of my, Father which is in heaven. Jesus did not say that it might be done. Jesus said that it would be done. Christ in You, The hope of Glory.** Just allow your Spirit, from God, within YOU to communicate with God its creator, within you let your Spirit, Re-born to God Communicate with its God Your Father. Communicating Spirit to Spirit, In Spirit and In Truth. Release your Faith from within your Spirit. **Enacting within you a personal spirit transformation from within. God almighty empowers us with the same power that "He" empowered Jesus with. Our transformation is an inner transformation, a transformation of our natural heart into a spirit heart, a heart in union and in communion with God.** A spirit heart that begins to grow within the grace of God. A Spiritual transformation taking place within our understanding as God wants us to understand. A spirit transformation that begins to teach us to rely on God Our Father. A Spirit transformation that teaches us to trust and have faith in God. A Spirit transformation that restores us to a place with God. A Spirit within the Kingdom of God that we as Human Spirits have never known before and could not ever have known in the natural, physical or material world. (Because this place was lost by Adam during the fall). **A place that our Spirit had with God in heaven before the foundation of the earth.** A spirit transformation that is based upon spirit intimacy (A love relationship with God) that was lost and now found and has its residency within the heart of each Spirit-Filled Believer. A Spirit transformation that brings about a knowing within the spirit heart of the Spirit-Filled Believer that he or she is safe within God's love. Because the Spirit-Filled Believer that dwells in God's love has the assurance of the reality of God. **Jesus says, I (A Spirit, God) will…manifest myself to him. "Manifest" means to make plain so Jesus says to the Spirit-filled Believer, "I will make myself real to you, you are a (Spirit) part of me." Jesus promises to make himself real to any Believer who will keep his commandments and Matthew 22:37-38 says, Jesus said unto him, thou shalt love the Lord thy God, with all thy heart, and with all they soul, and with all thy mind. This is the first and great commandment. And the second is like unto it, Thou shalt love thy neighbor as thyself."** Spirit-Filled Believers are called to know the real presence and reality of God. This is the love of God (Because God is love). Knowing this Spirit Love of God, we become spirit motivated to do those things that are fruitful to God and bring "Him" glory. This spirit transformation takes place within our hearts and begins to cause us to love the things that God loves and to hate the things that God hates. This spirit transformation that takes place within us begins to cause us to take on the mind of Jesus Christ. This spirit transformation that takes place within us causes us to want to be led by the resident Spirit of God within us the Holy Spirit. We begin to want to know more about God, the more we hunger and thirst for God. The more we then begin to be transformed within our Souls and Bodies into the image and likeness of God spiritually. It is at this point in your relationship with your Father, Jesus and the Holy Spirit that you have begun to become a threat to the Kingdom of Satan, which is not a natural kingdom here on this earth but a spiritual kingdom also, which wages a continual spiritual warfare. If you the Spirit-Filled Believer have not been taught about the spiritual battle which is taking place around you every day then, you are operating at a spiritual disadvantage. Because the warfare is a spirit battle, that has natural and material manifestations. This spirit battle is being fought against you using your own personal Spirit problems that came (Or that are being exposed) to you as you, the Spirit-Filled-Believer becomes closer to God. And the battle begins to escalate as you, Spirit-Filled Believer begin to crucify your own flesh becoming dead to sin. As you the Spirit Filled Believer begin to understand, accept and act upon your spiritual authority and spiritual power that is resident within you through the Gifts and Fruits of the Holy Spirit. Satan (A Spirit) will begin to target you specifically just like he did Jesus in the wilderness, because he understands that he has been judged and sentenced and that very soon that sentence will be carried out. That Jesus' promise of total transformation will be fully realized. The Devil understands better than you do that as a Spirit-Filled Believer, you are full of the Spirit of God. The devil and all that is evil understands that you have been called to **usher in God's Kingdom here on this earth, that you have the power resident within you for the destruction of "God's enemies. Satan** understands that you have been raised up **within the Spiritual realm and endued with**

spiritual power from on high and that you, yes; you will be instrumental in dislodging all of his spiritual powers and forces of evil. You see Satan knows and understands that spiritually **you are the Stronger Spirit, operating with all the authority of God resident within you. The same Spirit that raised Jesus, from the dead is operating within you, the same Spirit that is over all that is spiritually and naturally within this earth, under the earth and in heaven is operating within you. This is why you have to know who you are, why you were born-again and what you are here for, this is why you have to understand that you have to wage spiritual warfare. Your enemy Satan invisible to the natural eye is a spirit, his demons, fallen angels, evil and unclean spirits of bondage are invisible to the natural eyes because they are spirits, just like your Spirit is invisible to the natural eyes. Just like God is a Spirit, who is invisible to the natural eyes, but made visible to and through your eyes of faith your Spiritual eyes. Just like they that worship "Him" God, must worship "Him" in Spirit and in truth. Invisible to the natural eyes but realized and known through your spirit. Spirit-Filled-Believer, You are a Spirit sent from God to affect this earth, sent by God to usher in "His Kingdom" Matthew 6:10, Thy kingdom come. Thy will be done in earth, as it is in heaven.** You have to begin to take spirit responsibility and understand that your Spirit Man or Woman has been resurrected with the resurrection life of Jesus, The Holy Spirit and with the Holy Spirit came the Power of God within you, with power over all the power of the enemy. Satan knows that as long as he can secretly hide a spirit truth from you, he can inflict spirit hindrances, spirit cripplers and spirit strongholds within your soul or body. Satan knows that as long as you are blinded to what is within you cannot be as effective in the Kingdom of God as you should be. So he begins to inflict all sorts of spirit lies, spirit counterfeits, spirit distress and spirit and natural sickness within the inside of the Spirit-Filled-Believer's soul and body, thinking you will never look in the most obvious place of all the Spirit realm. All the while working his master plan to kill you, steal from you and destroy you with different harassment's and plagues. Satan does all of this dirty work from within the spirit realm. Then because he is so clever, cunning and deceptive he has us looking all over the world for the solutions and answers to the very things that he is either doing or has done, looking everywhere accept spiritually within the spirit realm where he knows that the Holy Spirit has already provided access to the answer. Looking around at everything and everybody, except himself and the fact that he could be acting spirit to spirit from within or spirit to spirit naturally from the outside to the inside as the source of the problem, situation or circumstance, either way he knows that it must be discerned that it is in fact a spirit problem that Satan has somehow perverted and is asserting spirit pressure through an enemy of God somehow. In Acts 13:13 The Apostle Paul addressing Elymas the sorcerer show us a clear picture of the devil's ability to pervert the things of God. "And said, O full of subtlety and all mischief, thou child of the devil, thou enemy of all righteousness, wilt thou not cease to pervert the right ways of the lord? 1 Peter 5:8 says, "Be sober, be vigilant, because your adversary the devil, as a roaring lion, walketh about seeking whom he may devour. Satan works unceasingly in his deadly, deceptive endeavors within the spirit realm on God's people. In Ecclesiastes 9:3 it says, "This evil among all things that are done under the sun, that there is one event unto all: yea, also the heart of the Sons of men is full of evil and madness is in their heart while they live, and after that they go to the dead." Satan utilizes the hearts of men and women, because he knows that our heart is the spirit center of our soul. In Acts 5:4 we can see Satan's deceptive and deadly work in the lives of some other New Testament Believers," But a certain man named Ananias, with Sapphira his wife sold a possession, and kept back part of the price, his wife also being privy to it, and brought a certain part and laid it at the Apostles feet. But Peter said, Ananias, why hath Satan filled thine heart to lie to the Holy Ghost and to keep back part of the price of the land? Whiles it remained, was it not thine own? And after it was sold was it not in thine own power? Why hast thou conceived this thing in thine heart? (Within the Spirit Realm) thou hast not lied unto men, but unto God. The Word of God says that it was the devil that put deceit into their hearts and that it was done through the spirit realm not in the natural. John 13:2 says "And supper being ended, the devil having now put it into the heart of Judas Iscariot, Simon's son to betray him. (Working within the spirit realm.) Evil is being launched at the people of God from within the spiritual realm and it is damaging the men and women of God, Spiritually, Physically, Mentally and Emotionally. Demonic influence is working against God's people through the use of Transference of Spirits, Hindering Spirits, Unclean Spirits, Familiar Spirits, Witchcraft Spirits and many other Spiritual forces, including Sins, Iniquities and Transgressions. Here on this earth real Spirit warfare is waged against us and Jesus came to destroy the works of the devil. 1John 3:8" For this purpose the Son of God was manifested, that he might destroy the works of the devil. And to set the captives free, proclaiming liberty, taking away the pain of the brokenhearted, Jesus proclaiming, "The Spirit of The Lord God is upon me; because the Lord hath anointed me to preach good tidings unto the meek; he hath sent me to bind up the brokenhearted, to proclaim liberty to the captives, and the opening of the prison to them that are bound…to comfort all that mourn; to appoint unto them that mourn in Zion to give unto them beauty for ashes, the oil of joy for mourning, the garment of praise for the spirit of heaviness." These are the very same verses that Jesus quoted when announcing to the Church why he had come. Whether the people that Jesus ministered to were victims of direct demonic attack of evil or spirit abuse resulting in evil, Jesus seemed to see people as those who had been overpowered. Jesus' part then and now was and is to Set-Them-Free. Jesus said speaking of himself that Satan had no power over him or any rights over him. Jesus said in John 14:30 "Hereafter, I will not talk much with you; for the prince of this world cometh and hath nothing in me." And Jesus desires that we be as free from the Evil and Demonic influences of Satan as he himself was here on this earth. Jesus brought freedom and peace to people being hit by demons, evil spirits and their demonic influence. The Apostle Paul spoke about a messenger of Satan, sent to Buffet him, the definition of Buffet according to the American Heritage Dictionary of the English Language, 3rd Edition©1999 is to hit or beat, especially repeatedly. To strike forcefully; to batter, to force one's way with difficulty or to drive or force with repeated blows (is this sounding in any way remotely familiar to you) even unto this present day Paul said, in 2 Corinthians 12:7, think about this, he is speaking here specifically about a Spirit, a spiritual messenger of Satan, dispatched upon a spirit mission, dispatched through, from or within the spirit realm. A messenger Spirit dispatched spiritually, against a man of God, to operate negatively against him here on this earth within the natural, physical or the earthly realm, no one knows exactly how this Spirit was operating, but one thing for sure we know Paul wanted to be rid of it. Today we to as spirit beings can no longer deny that both of these realms exist. And guess what that doesn't make us weird, strange, crazy or super spiritual to acknowledge the truth, whether we like it or not, that's just the way it is. Which means that we can no longer just operate in one realm while ignoring the other? Man was made by God to be able to operate in both the Spirit or Heavenly realm and the Natural or Physical realm at the same time. Satan knows that as well as God does, how can I know that you ask because the Word of God tells us in Ephesians 6:12 " For we wrestle not against flesh and blood, but against powers, against the rulers of the darkness of this world, against **Spiritual Wickedness in high places,** there is a spirit battle going on right now within the spirit realm between the forces of righteousness, God's Angels, good spirits and the forces of evil, Spirits fallen hosts and part of our calling as Spirit-Filled Believers, empowered by The Holy Spirit is to Fight the good fight of faith, lay hold on eternal life, whereunto thou art also called and hast professed a good profession before many witnesses. The Chief goal of the Evil Spirits is to hinder, slow down what is absolutely going to happen, with the soon coming return of Our Lord and Savior Jesus Christ.

Because You Are a Spirit, Spirits Fight You

Evil Spirits interfere on every realm that they can, waging spiritual warfare on the people of God. This warfare is enacted within the spiritual realm of the heavenlies, here on earth and within the Soulish and Physical realm. All in an attempt of Evil to thwart the plans and purposes of God, including your role in God's plan, because you have always been in the plans and purposes of God. Jesus was physically buffeted, and we know and understand that Jesus suffered many indignities on "His" way to Calvary. The Word of God says in Matthew 26:67 "Then did they spit in his face and buffeted him. **When Jesus rose from the dead Jesus conquered death, hell, the grave and the power of sin, the Word of God, speaking of the Apostle Paul says that he was full of the Holy Spirit, full of the wisdom of God, full of the Power of God, full of the Love of God and full of the light of the revelation of Jesus Christ.** And the Apostle Paul said in 2 Corinthians 12:7 "And lest I should be exalted above measure through the abundance of the revelations, there was given to me a thorn in the flesh, the messenger of Satan to Buffet Me, lest I should be exalted above measure." Again The Apostle Paul said in 1 Corinthians 11; 4 "Even unto this present hour we both hunger and thirst, and are naked, and are buffeted and have no certain dwelling place." Paul, the Apostle of joy, courage, steadfastness, faithfulness, endurance, patience and love. Paul, the servant of God who's entire life was a life of consecration had to contend with a specific spiritual situation. The Apostle Paul was buffeted by a Messenger of Satan. We have invisible spiritual enemies and foes. God told us in Ephesians 6:12" For we wrestle not against flesh and blood, but against principalities, against powers, against the rulers of the darkness of this world, **"Against spiritual wickedness in high places"** Let me ask you a couple of questions here, why has God given us assurances over spiritual forces as well as natural forces? In Luke 10:19, Jesus is talking to us 'Behold, I give unto you power to tread on serpents and scorpions, and over all the power of the enemy: and nothing shall by any means hurt you. (Both naturally and spiritually is the given expression here) But too many of us continue to look for all of the answers to everything in the natural realm. Time out for that now, we have to look within the spiritual realm also. This spiritual warfare that we are engaged in is taking place outside of the realm of our natural consciousness. There is also a Godly battle that is taking place within the spiritual realm with manifestations in both the spiritual and natural realms. In this spiritual battle that is taking place. Our Born-Again Spiritual man or woman is seeking to over power, or to dethrone, our souls and our flesh through the power of the Holy Spirit. This process is called sanctification 1 Thessalonians 5:23 says, "And the very God of peace sanctify you wholly; and I pray God your whole Spirit, and Soul and Body be preserved blameless unto the coming of our Lord Jesus Christ." Sanctification, as used in the Word of God means to make holy, to consecrate, to separate from the world. And be set apart from sin in order that we may have close fellowship with God and serve him. The scriptural standard of sanctification as expressed in Matthew 22:37-38 "Jesus said unto him, thou shalt love the Lord thy God with all thy heart, and with all thy Soul, and with all thy Mind. This is the first and great commandment. Sanctification, perfecting holiness as in 2 Corinthians 7:1, "Having therefore these promises, dearly beloved, let us cleanse ourselves from all filthiness of the flesh and spirit, perfecting holiness in the fear of God. Sanctification as in 1 Timothy 1:5 "Now the end of the commandment is charity out of a pure heart, and of a good conscience, and of faith unfeigned." Sanctification as in Philippians 1:10 "That ye may approve things that are excellent that ye may be sincere and without offense till the day of Christ. Sanctification as in Romans 6:18 "Being then made free from sin, ye became the servants of righteousness." Sanctification as in Romans 6:19" I speak after the manner of men because of the infirmity of your flesh, for as ye have yielded your members servants to uncleanness. And to iniquity unto iniquity; even so now yield your members servants to righteousness unto holiness. Sanctification as in 1 John 3:22 "And whatsoever we ask, we receive of him, because we keep his commandments, and do those things that are pleasing in his sight. Sanctification as in 1 John 5:4 "For whatsoever is born of God overcometh the world: and this is the victory that overcometh the world, even our faith. Who is he that overcometh the world, but he that believeth that Jesus is the Son of God. This scripture describes the operation of the Holy Spirit through salvation in Jesus Christ by which "He" delivers us from the slavery and power of sin. Separating us from the sinful practices of this present world. Renewing our nature according to the image of Jesus Christ, producing the fruit of the Spirit and enabling us to live a holy and victorious life of dedication to God. Jesus has promised us that "His" authority, Power and presence will accompany us as we battle the kingdom of Satan, Evil and Demonic Influence and liberate people from the captivity to evil. Satan (A Spirit, a Transformed Angel whose name was Lucifer) the epitome and personification of everything unholy and evil continually wages spiritual warfare against the Spirit-Filled Believers on the earthly realm and within the spiritual realm. Unfortunately today, too many Spirit-Filled Believers are mistakenly, openly and willfully, accepting the bad and unpleasant spiritual calamities, situations and circumstances that the enemy has targeted and tormented them with daily. We are accepting them as not coming from within the spirit realm from the Devil and Evil hosts, we seem to be accepting them as negative situations or evil circumstances that are supposed to be happening to us. (We then are accepting these unseen spirits and spirit forces, operating in disguise.) These are however Evil Spirits, Demons and Demonic Spirit forces operating, within the spirit realm spirit forces and Spirits, which have been Set- up for and against us, by Evil spirit enemies. Spirits, Demons and Evil Spirit forces that have been Set-up to work against our lives so that we will be full of spirit limitations, thereby causing our spirit wills to be continually contained within a narrow and limited spirit understanding. At this point what begins to take place within the life of a Spirit-Filled Believer is that you will begin to flee from **The Spirit Wholeness and Completeness that God has ordained for you and me.** We do this by unconsciously monitoring ourselves to make sure that we don't go to far away from our comfortable, known religious zones that are not really comfortable, but as long as we stay there we wrongly believe that we don't have to feel any new or additional pain or suffering other than what our resident evil, demonic, inner negative spirit forces have been and are continually inflicting upon us. **In reality what you have allowed to happen is you have accepted and you have become accustomed to those Evil Spirits, Demons and their Demonic Influence operating against you even to the point that they have begun to see through you, feel through you, talk through you and even act through you. In fact those Evil Spirits, Demons and Demonic Influence have gone so far as to have tricked you into believing that what you think is actually you are them. This happens because you have become so accustomed to their negative inner and many times outward spirit projections, forcing their pain and suffering on you to the point that pain and suffering doesn't even feel like pain or suffering to you any more, its as if they have become to us something that is just there. Misery, pain negativity and sorrow when it gets to this point in your spirit life whether those Evil Spirits, Demons and Demonic Influence are known to your spirit or not they are in operation.** (Hence, generational curses, spoken curses, spirits that have entered in from the womb, cultural curses, religious spirits, hindering spirits, unclean spirits, familiar spirits, transferring of spirits and witchcraft spirits.) **For the most part all of us have a healthy spirit self, from a worldly perspective that is. A self that is capable of the everyday functions that are considered normal, such as being independent, setting and attaining goals, experiencing intimacy and enjoying the moment. In most people to a significant degree, and in some people to a very large degree. We see what appears to be a spiritually healthy and happy, Spirit-Filled Believer.** Spirit problems cannot be seen with the natural eye, while this outwardly apparently healthy Spirit-Filled Believer appears whole and happy. When in reality they are experiencing spirit problems they will begin to treat every task as if it were a catastrophe waiting to happen. Those Evil Spirits, Demons and their Demonic Influence will cause the person with spirit problems to have a sense of humor that is full of bitterness, causing them to look at and to experience what is supposed to be a good, happy and joyful situation with negative feelings masked by false dutiful smiles and many times fake forced laughter, remember that those forces are working through the person, with or without their knowledge. Those Evil Spirits, Demons and Demonic Influence have them living in a kind of spirit prison or what is known as spirit bondage. The born-again Spirit-Filled Believers Spirit, being filled with The Holy Spirit is fighting spirit warfare. That is being waged within the inside of the body of that believer. In fact an actual war is raging, an invisible war within the Mind, Soul and Body of that Spirit-Filled Believer that can produce tangible effects. And the manifestations of the effects, from that type of spirit warfare is then experienced by the Spirit-Filled Believer in various forms within them mind, their soul, their will, their emotions, their intellect and from within their natural body as pain, disease, sickness and torment. If these problems are not recognized as spiritual and dealt with from a biblical and spirit perspective they can produce devastating effects within the life of a Spirit-Filled Believer. **And guess what else? No! They don't just disappear and go away as many Spirit-Filled Believers have been wrongly taught to believe.** Evil Spirits, Demons and Demonic Influences can and do cause many spirit problems that reveal themselves by manifesting as natural problems that can go unanswered for the Spirit-Filled Believer. A major tactic of the enemy is many times when the Spirit-Filled Believers are battling within this arena of spirit warfare they can and do experience or re-experience at times measures of spirit freedom and victory. Spirit freedom and victory such as they felt when Jesus first became Lord of their live or when he or she first became born-again. It is experienced something like this: Suddenly the Spirit-Filled Believer begins to feel unusually good about their life in Jesus Christ. Feeling good about them selves and feeling joyful both spiritually and naturally. Happy to be alive both spiritually and naturally enjoying each moment of the day and savoring their lives being led by the Spirit of God. They at this point and time within are spirit alive to God. Many times this experience only occurs within them while they are in church, in prayer or around other Spirit-Filled Believers. Then very often with very little awareness of how or what is happening to them they slip back into their old previous heavy warring state of spirit bondage's that they had been previously experiencing. The Spirit-Filled Believer although having a God consciousness will have a feeling within them that there is more available to them than what they seem to have or are experiencing with God. The relationship seems to be in and out, up and down never permanent or long lasting, almost as if seemingly never to escape from their own personal feelings of why the drought, the lack, why is the struggle so hard for me, what is the reason for these feelings of sorrow, helplessness and why do I have such an inability to perceive what is going on with me in what I am experiencing. All of this while trying to obtain and maintain a consistent level of personal spiritual victory. To many times trying to rationalize and understand what is our own spirit dilemma, trying to use natural measuring standards, exclusive of Holy Spirit revelation of the Word of God, because those Evil Spirits, Demons and Demonic Influence have created a Demonic fog that is fogging everything up within their soul trying to cover up and squeeze out the Holy Spirit. At this point again the Spirit-Filled Believer, not realizing that they have now opened themselves up to a whole new can of spirit serpents and scorpions. Causing the Spirit-Filled Believer to become confronted by an additional group of Evil Spirits, Demons and Demonic Influences. Spirits that are going to cause them more spirit problems and discomfort. Some of the problems and discomfort are and were in fact part of the originally inherited, unrecognized spirit problems that had been warring with their soul and or body from the beginning of your new life as a Spirit-Filled Believer. Broken marriages; abused children, addictions, acts of abuse or violence that people direct against you and you may have directed toward others; desperate yearnings for money, power, celebrity status and in many cases living corrupt lies and loving it. Experiencing symptoms that can include, perverse sexual fascination; unnatural visions of grandiosity, real or imagined feelings of persecutions, hero fantasies played out through video games and unnatural power plays sometimes also played out in unrealistic situations within our own souls. Desires to make other people experience guilt, jealousy and manipulation, collecting and spewing out false and surmised accusations, always experiencing foreboding feelings of disaster or pending doom, never anything good, engaging in strange superstitions and religious rituals. Fostering real or unreal threats of attack, torture, loss of love, loss of control, loss of temper, loss of support, fears and fear of death. Thus many Spirit-Filled Believers are stuck trying to defend themselves within this unnatural spirit battleground. Trying to defend yourself utilizing natural tactics in a spirit battleground. Trying to do what cannot be done due to a failure on the part of the Spirit-Filled Believer to recognize that the warfare that is raging is Evil, Demonic and Spirits. Failing to realize that what is taking place is coming from within the spirit realm and many times from within and not always stemming from without. Failing to see in the spirit realm that the sources are completely under the control of and being monitored by Evil Spirits, Demons and Demonic Influence. Satan the enemy of God and his Demonic host, the enemy of everything that is Godly and Good. Evil, Spirits, Demons, Demonic Influence that seem to appear (although invisible to the natural eye, because they are spirit) and feel like they are a natural spirit jailer. Enemy forces that are continually waging spirit warfare with each and every Spirit-Filled Believer, trying to seduce and bewitch them to a state of lack of faith in God, and in "His" Word. Evil Spirits and demonic Influence threatens us with poverty and lack so that our confidence in God's ability to provide for us will weaken, and inevitably be stolen from us. All this in Evils continual attempts to try and make us sin against God, thus trying to make us lose our souls and be led to death and hell, attempting over and over again by waging an invisible spirit warfare against us from within the spirit realm, buffeting us and then retreating and hiding. The devil's goal is that you succumb to spirit bondage, while in bondage become object fixated on your problems, negative situations and circumstances, thus making it seem to you that you are in a life drama that is being played out within your mind, will, emotions and intellect (the soulish realm.) causing your mind, your thoughts, your will, your emotions and your body to become wrongly focused, causing you to misperceive and wrongly project into every situation that comes up in your life, causing you to remember, re-enact and many times re-live the same negative things over and over again. The Spirit-Filled Believer then begins to question and up springs doubt, unbelief and wondering within his or her own mind and makes them sometimes ask themselves the age old question Why me? Our very human nature and our born-again spirit questions why? You say why would our born-again spirit question why? Simply because your born-again regenerated spirit knows through the Holy Spirit of God which it is a part of that what is happening to you within your spirit is not according to the will of God's best for "His" child. The Holy Spirit knows that those Evil Spirits, Demons and Demonic Influences will cause the Spirit-Filled Believer to take on a false spirits, of self that can become self-negating, self-destroying, self-limiting, self-effacing, self-protecting, self-involved, self-aggrandizing and cause you to be forever falsely trying to bolster a fragile false (spirit evil spirit endued) self-esteem. This is in reality another Spirit Dilemma. Now you have operating: A self-interfering spirit, now also interfering with the born-again resident spirit of God. Making you to feel as if you are continually being buffeted and in fact you are experiencing just that continual buffeting. I want you to understand something the Holy Spirit within you knows that those spirits and spiritual forces are exactly what's causing you not to be able to reach your own personal level of the Victorious Life Promised through, the Lord Jesus Christ. This may be your situation up to now, but I want you to understand that you can be set-free, delivered, victory can be yours now, In The name of Jesus. You have the authority and the power to stop all of that buffeting with all of its negativism, torment, pain and suffering, those feeling that have caused you to feel as if you have been on a spiritual roller coaster ride and confused. You can get rid of those spiritual problems that you, didn't even realize were and are hindering and holding you back from experiencing the joyful, happy, peaceful, loving and victorious life that has been guaranteed to you through the shed blood of Jesus at Calvary. The Word of God brings to nothing spiritual problems, strongholds and destroys spiritual principalities and spirits enabling a person to be transformed to the glory of God

Because You Are a Spirit,
Spirits Work to Block and Obstruct You

This has been revealed to us in the Word of God by the Apostle Paul in Gal. 5:7, but because it was not specifically called a Spirit we have over looked the vile nature, character, deeds, and the opposing actions of this Spirit. Gal. 5:7 says, "Ye did run well; who did Hinder you that ye should not obey the truth. The Apostle Paul while on his Missionary Journey had gone to Thessalonica, a seaport trade center. Paul ministered here some Jews and many Greek proselytes believed, but the opposition became so strong that Paul found it necessary to leave. In writing back to the church in Thessalonica, in 1 Thess. 2:18, The Apostle says, "Wherefore we would have come unto you, even I Paul, once and again; But Satan Hindered us. The name Satan in the Greek form is a derivative from the Aramaic, Satanas'as and is defined as; an adversary. This the second name given to the prince of the devils. The other name is diabolos, Devil and look at its definition; the one who casts either himself or something else between two in order to separate them. The false accuser in his name as Satan, he is the Opposer. In Matt. 40 it says, "Then saith, Jesus unto him, "Get thee hence, Satan for it is written, Thou shalt worship the Lord thy God, and Him only shalt thou serve. In Mark 1:13 it says, "And he was there in the wilderness forty days, tempted of Satan; and was with the wild beasts; and the angels ministered unto him. Satanas' is the prince of the fallen angels, and is also used collectively as a word for Evil Spirits or devils. Satan the adversary, Satan the Opposer, the satanic kingdom is active in this world, attacking God's people with the express purpose of taking advantage of as many people as possible and as often as possible. Satan and his co-horts love operating from within the inside of people. From within the inside of a person there is a greater advantage in controlling them. If his attack is successful it will cause you and I to have less love and a hardened heart toward God and your fellow Christians. Gal. 5:7 says, "Ye did run well; who did Hinder you that ye should not obey the truth?" Who did Hinder you? 1

Thess. 2:18" Wherefore we would have come unto you, even I Paul, once and again; But Satan Hindered us. I want to make this very clear and try to provide you with an example of an attempt by Satan to use the forces of Hindering Spirits and Forces in an attempt to oppose God's divine plan of salvation and redemption for you and I. In Matt. 16:13-19 it says "When Jesus came into the coasts of Caesare' Philippi, he asked his disciple, saying "Whom do men say that I the Son of Man, am? And they said, some say that thou art John the Baptist; some Elias; and other, Jeremias, or one of the prophets. He saith unto them, "But whom say ye that I am? And Simon Peter answered and said, "Thou art the Christ, the Son of the Living God." And Jesus answered and said unto him, "Blessed art thou, Simon Barjona: for flesh and blood hath not revealed it unto thee, but my Father which is in heaven. And I say also unto thee, that thou art Peter, and upon this rock, I will build my Church; and the gates of hell shall not prevail against it. And I will give unto thee the keys of the kingdom of heaven: and whatsoever thou shalt bind on earth shall be bound in heaven: and whatsoever thou shalt loose on earth shall be loosed in heaven: and whatsoever thou shalt loose on earth shall be loosed in heaven. Then charged he his disciples that they should tell no man that he was Jesus Christ. From that time forth began Jesus to shew unto his disciples, how that he must go unto Jerusalem, and suffer many things of the elders and chief priests and scribes, and be killed and be raised against the third day. Then Peter took him, and began to rebuke him (Jesus) saying (God forbid) be it far from thee, Lord: this shall not be unto thee. But he turned, and said unto Peter. "Get thee behind me, Satan: thou art an offence unto me: for thou savourest not the things that be of God, but those that be of men. Here is a perfect example of a Hindering Spirit, a Spirit unloosed speaking through Peter in an attempt to Oppose or Hinder the divine plan of God for man's salvation and redemption by Jesus Christ's suffering and death on the cross, Jesus identified this Spirit as Satan. In The Word of God in the book of Zechariah in the 3rd Chapter, Satan's strategy is revealed to Zechariah the prophet, concerning Joshua the high priest in a vision from God, where after the exile he would Hinder the reinstitution of the divine worship, asserting that Israel is rejected by the just judgment of God and is not worthy of the renewal of the priest hood. In Zechariah 3:1-2 it says, "And he showed me Joshua the priest standing before the angel of the Lord and Satan standing at this right hand to resist him. And the Lord said unto Satan. **The Lord Rebuke thee, O Satan,** even the Lord that hath chosen Jerusalem rebuke thee: is no this a brand plucked out of the fire. "As we continue to read and recount the chapter, we find that the filthy garments are stripped off the high priest, and that the high priest receives festal garments instead with the declaration that his sins are taken away. **Joshua the high priest standing before the Angel of the Lord, and Satan standing at his right hand to resist him (To Hinder) standing before the presence of the Angel of the Lord. The Lord rebuked Satan and refused to permit him to stop the restoration of Judah and Jerusalem. Twice Satan was rebuked.** Who knows exactly, Joshua evidently ministering in garments that were not holy or proper of high priests. His filthy garments were taken away, his iniquity was cleansed, and he was clothed with the appropriate attire. The high priests miter was also placed upon his head. Then the angel that stood by gave him a charge concerning conditions he should meet to be the high priest and be blessed.

After that he was given a prophecy regarding the coming of the messiah and the salvation. In Romans 1:10-13 The Amplified Bible. The Apostle Paul's Epistle to the Saints in Rome "I keep pleading that somehow by God's will I may now at last prosper and come to you. For I am yearning to see you, that I may impart and share with you some Spiritual Gift to strengthen and establish you. That is, that we may be mutually strengthened and encouraged and comforted by each other's faith, both yours and mine. I want you to know, brethren, that many times, I have planned and intended to come to you though thus far, I have been Hindered and Prevented, in order that I might have some fruit (some results of my labors) among you, as I have among the rest of the Gentiles. In Romans 15:19-22, The Amplified Bible, it says, "Even as my preaching has been accompanied with the power of signs and wonders, and all of it by the power of the Holy Spirit. The result is that starting from Jerusalem and as far round as Illyricum, I have fully preached the gospel faithfully executing, accomplishing, carrying out to the full the good news of Christ the Messiah in its entirety. Thus my ambition has been to preach the gospel, not where Christ's name has already been known, lest I build on another man's foundation; but instead I would act on the principle as it is written, they shall see who have never been told of Him, and they shall understand who have never heard of him. This ambition is the reason why I have so frequently been Hindered, from coming to visit you. Verse 29 And I know that when I do come to you, I shall come in the Abundant Blessings of the gospel of Christ." Satan tried to Hinder the Ministry of Jesus. In Matt. 4:1-11 it says "Then was Jesus led up of the Spirit into the wilderness to be tempted of the devil. And when he had fasted forty days and forty nights he was afterward an hungered. And when the tempter came to him, he said If thou be the Son of God, command that these stones be made bread. But he answered and said, it is written, Man shall not live by bread alone, but by every word that proceedeth out of the mouth of God. Then the devil taketh him up into the holy city, and setteth him on a pinnacle of the temple. And saith unto him, If thou be the Son of God, cast thyself down: for it is written, he shall give his angels charge concerning thee: and in their hands they shall bear thee up, lest at anytime thou dash thy foot against a stone. Jesus, said unto him, It is written again, thou shalt not tempt the Lord thy God. Again, the devil taketh him up into an exceeding high mountain, and sheweth him all the kingdoms of the world, and the glory of them; and saith unto him, all these things will I give thee, if thou wilt fall down and worship me. Then saith Jesus unto him, "Get thee hence, Satan: for it is written, Thou shalt worship the Lord they God, and him only shalt thou serve. Then the devil leaveth him, and, behold Angels came and ministered unto him. Satan tried to Hinder Jesus from Completing His Ministry. In Matt. 16:22-23 it says, "Then Peter took Him (Jesus) and began to rebuke him saying, be it far from thee, Lord: this shall not be unto thee. But He turned, and said unto Peter, "Get thee behind me, Satan, thou art an offence unto me: for thou savourest not the things that be of God, but those that be of men. HINDERING SPIRIT. By now you are surely asking yourself why would these hindering Spirits want to hinder me? Why not you? Hindering Spirits tried to hinder Jesus Christ the Son of God and some Hindering Spiritual forces actually did hinder the Apostle Paul. And the reason that you and I have been harassed and our full Blessing's have not come forth is that you and I are not just some face less, no name little person to the devil. The devil knows what we are better than some of us do. He knows the Spirit Power and the Spirit Authority that we possess over him and his kingdom. The enemy knows all about our sin nature too, he knows your name, your telephone number, your address, your email address, your friends, your enemies and which buttons work to torment you, block you, harass and hinder you when pushed. The enemy knows your fears and your strongholds and knowing this he formulates and begins to customize a specialized attack just for you. Satan is no dummy, he knows full well that your weaknesses, strongholds and your lack of knowledge is his only edge against you. Hindering Spirit Forces can actually be used by the enemy to become barriers, walls, or obstacles and road blocks to impede personal relationships with the Lord Jesus Christ. Hindering Spirits can block and obstruct our receiving revelation from God and they can temporarily block us from receiving answers to our prayer. **Please understand that the reason that some of you have not received your blessings of the fulfillment of your destiny in Jesus Christ and prosperity is that these Hindering Spirits and Forces may be in operation. Hindering Spirits can be unloosed by Witches. These Spirits can Hinder your personal Spirit growth as well as Church. Hindering Spirits can cause your faith to go shipwreck because they have the ability to put so much unidentifiable havoc in and around a person's life, causing them to many times doubt God's ability. There are Hindering Spirits of resistance that can operate within a person's life that can actually cause an individual to resist the truth of The Word of God and the Holy Spirit. These Hindering Spirits can cause an individual to resist, salvation, deliverance, praise, worship, prayer and healing. Hindering Spirits and Forces can bring on sickness, family breakdowns, poverty, defeat, secular religious and people disfavor. Hindering Spirits love to operate through and by negative and oppressive demonic talk or confessions coming out of the mouth of another believer or friend. You see negative words that are either spoken, written or thought against another person can become supernatural darts of negative spiritual power which tends to continue to operate through time until they are either broken, renounced, rebuked, or broken off of the life of a person Hindering Spirits, operating in the life of a person will cause them to be the tail and not the head, which is contrary to the Word of God.** These Hindering Spirits and Forces can produce humiliation in the life of the person that they are operating in and they can produce Spirit forces of failure to reproduce. Physically, Mentally, Emotionally, Financially and Spiritually. All Hindering Spirits and Hindering Forces are works of the Devil. 1 John 3:8 says, "For this purpose the Son of God was manifested, that he might destroy the works of the devil. The word of God says, 2 Cor. 1:10 "Who delivered us from so great a death, (Past) and doth deliver; (Present) in whom we trust that He (Jesus) will yet Deliver us (future) Psalm 34:19 says, "Many are the afflictions of the righteous; but the Lord Delivereth Him out of them all.

"But He that is joined unto the Lord is one Spirit"
"Do you not know that you are the Temple of God?
And that the Spirit of God dwells in you?
If anyone defiles the Temple of God,
God will destroy him, for the Temple of God is Holy,
Which Temple You Are.
1 Corinthians 3: 16, 17
And again" Or do you not know that your
Body is the Temple of The Holy Spirit who is in you,
WHOM YOU HAVE FROM GOD
And you are not your own?
For you were bought at a price;
Therefore Glorify God In
Your Body and in Your Spirit,
Which are God's
1 Corinthians 6: 19, 20

Because You Are a Spirit,

There Can be a Transference of Spirits Every Spirit-filled believer should be able to accept and understand the ability of Spirits to transfer. The greatest **Transference of a Spirit that ever happened took place in the book of Acts Chapter 2 verses 1-4 which says, "And when the day of Pentecost was fully come, they were all with one accord in one place. And suddenly there came a sound from heaven as of a rushing mighty wind, and it filled all the house where they were sitting. And there appeared unto hem cloven tongues like as of fire, and it sat upon each of them. And they were all filled with the Holy Ghost, and began to speak with other tongues, as The Spirit gave them utterance. That is the same Spirit that was transferred upon you and me, when we received Jesus into our hearts as our Lord and Savior, the same Spirit that baptizes us in to Jesus and fills us with the power of God, in order to be a witness of Jesus.** One dictionary definition of the word Transfer is; to pass from one place, person or thing to another. Transference is: The act or process of transferring. The secular world of psychoanalysis defines Transference as the process by which emotions and desires originally associated with one person, such as a parent or sibling, are unconsciously shifted to another person. The world knows that emotions and desires can be shifted or transferred to another person. We know that this is impossible in the natural realm, because this is a spiritual occurrence, and it may explain why two children raised in the same house with the same training can turn out so differently. As in Luke 15:11-

32, "And he said, A certain man had two sons; and the youngest of them said to his father, Father, give me the portion of good that falleth to me. And he divided unto them his journey into a far country, and there wasted his substance with riotous living. And when he had spent all, there arose a mighty famine in that land; and he begin to be in want. And he went and joined himself to a citizen of that country; and he sent him into his fields to feed swine. And he would fain have filled his belly with the husks that the swine did eat: And no man gave unto him, **and when he came to himself.** He said How many hired servants of my father's have bread enough and to spare, and I perish with hunger. **The Word of God, just says, He came to himself,** came to himself, meaning he must not have been himself. Verse 18, I will arise and go to my father, and will say unto him father; I have sinned against heaven, and before thee. And am no more worthy to be called thy son; make me as one of thy hired servants. And he arose, and came to his father. But when he was yet a great way off, his father saw him, and had compassion, and ran, and fell on his neck, and kissed him. And the son said unto him, Father, I have sinned against heaven, and in thy sight, and am no more worthy to be called thy son. But the father said to his servants, bring forth the best robe, and put it on him; and put a ring on his hand, and shoes on his feet: And bring hither the fatted calf, and kill it; and let us eat, and be merry: For this my son was dead, **and is alive again; He was lost and is found.** And they began to be merry. Now his elder son was in the field: and as he came and drew nigh to the house, he heard music and dancing. And he called one of the servants, and asked what these things mean and he said unto him, thy brother is come; and thy father hath killed the fatted calf, because he hath received him safe and sound. And he was angry, and would not go in: therefore came his father out, and entreated him. (The other son and brother) And he answering said to his father, lo, these many years do I serve thee, neither transgressed I at any time thy commandment: And yet thou never gavest me a kid, that I might make merry with my friends: But as soon as this thy son was come, which hath devoured thy living with harlots, thou has killed for him the fatted calf. And he said unto him, Son, thou are ever with me, and all that I have is thine. It was meet that we should make merry, and be glad; for this thy brother was dead, **and is alive again: and was lost, and is found.** Two brothers, raised in the same home with the same training, yet they turned out so differently. Could this situation of spirits so different account for so much division in homes, friendships and fellowships? **Transference of Spirits is scriptural. In the book of Numbers, Chapter 11: We have an example of God enacting Transference of the powerful anointing of Moses unto the seventy elders.** In Numbers 11:16,17,24,25; "And the Lord said unto Moses, gather unto me seventy men of the elders of Israel, whom thou knowest to be the elders of the people, and officers over them; and bring them unto the tabernacle of the congregation, that they may stand there with thee. And I will come down and talk with thee **there**: And I will take of the Spirit which is upon thee, and will put it upon them; and they shall bear the burden of the people with thee, that thou bear it not thyself alone. Verse 24, 25, And Moses went out, and told the people the words of the Lord, and gathered the seventy men of the elders of the people, and set them round about the tabernacle, and the Lord came down in a cloud, and spake unto him, and **took of the Spirit that was upon him (Moses) and gave it unto the** seventy elders: **And it came to pass that when The Spirit rested upon them, they prophesied, and did not cease. God first implemented Transference of Spirits for "His" purpose for Good. Now I want to illustrate to you the Transference of Evil Spirits.** In the book of Genesis, Chapter 19: It describes how, the two Angels arrived at Sodom and rescued Lot, his daughters and his wife. Sodom and Gomorrah had Spirits of rebellion and perversion prevailing within. Sodom was a rebellious land, 1 Samuel 15:23 says, "For rebellion is as the sin of witchcraft, and stubbornness is as iniquity and idolatry." The basic sin of witchcraft is rebellion against the commandments of God. Instead of choosing God's way choosing to go their own way, doing their own thing without submitting to God's authority or consulting God. The Spirit of rebellion opened the doors for the spirits of disobedience, perversions, captivity to Satan, lust, deceit, anti-submissivess to God and every evil work. In Sodom and Gomorrah, The Spirit of the World, this is the Spirit of Satan. Verse 26 says, "But his wife looked back from behind him, and she became a pillar of salt." **The Spirit of Sodom and Gomorrah had transferred on Lot's wife;** she submitted her will to those Sprits. But it doesn't end there. Those same Sprits had Transferred on Lot's daughters also, but manifested later through rebellion on the part of Lot's daughters, resulting in incest. Verses 30-31; Lot's daughters got him drunk and had sex with their father. **What we have here is an example of Transference of Evil Spirits.** I want to give you another example of the Transference of Evil Spirits. In the book of Numbers, Chapter 13: It tells us how Moses sent twelve men to spy out the land God had promised to Israel. Ten of these spies returned with a negative report. They told of great walled cities and a powerful enemy within the land. **Those ten spies transferred a Spirit of Fear and Unbelief to the rest of God's people.** "They said, we are not able to go up against the people for they are stronger than we…There we saw the giants…and we were like grasshoppers in our own sight and so we were in their sight." This report caused Israel to fail to obey the command of God, subsequently; many did not see the Promised Land. **Two of the spies however, had a different Spirit, In Numbers 14: it says,"** And Joshua the son of Num and Caleb the son of Jephunneh, who were among those who had spied out the land, tore their clothes; and they spoke to all the congregation of the children of Israel, saying:"The land we passed through to spy out is an exceedingly good land. If the Lord delights in us, then He will bring us into this land and give it to us, a land which flows with milk and honey." Caleb and Joshua beseeched the people not to rebel against God, not to have fear. **Two different sets of Spirits were seeking to control the people; one set was the Spirit of Rebellion against God, fear, doubt, unbelief, and cowardice. The other Spirit was the Spirit of God, spoken through Caleb and Joshua." Let us go up at once, and possess the land: For we are well able to overcome it." Numbers 13:30,** But look at how the negative Spirits of the ten spies affected the people. So all the congregation lifted up their voices and cried, and the people wept that night. And all the children of Israel complained against Moses and Aaron, and the whole congregation said to them," If only we had died in the land of Egypt: or if only we had died in this wilderness: why has the Lord brought us to this land to fall by the sword, that our wives and children should become victims? Would it not be better for us to return to Egypt? "So they said to one another," Let us select a leader and return to Egypt. (Numbers 14:1-4)

These were the Spirits of Rebellion, murmuring, despair, fear, doubt and unbelief that had transferred among God's people. God's people were not kept out of the Promised Land because of n inferior army, but because of a Wrong Spirit. Why were the people affected by the Evil Spirits instead of the Good Spirits? Our **sin nature tends to immediately accept and believe an Evil report and we tend to follow the crowd.** If the children of Israel had accepted the Good Report, they would have had to expos themselves to great danger. **Our human nature always wants to take the easy way. According to the Word of God another form of Evil Transference of Spirits that takes place is through the laying on of hands.** In 1Timothy 5:22 it says, lay hands suddenly on no man, neither be partaker of other men's sins: keep thy self pure. According to this passage of scripture we must be sure of the individual that lays hands on us. God approves and sanctions the laying on of hands for the Transference of Good and Godly purposes because, "His" word says in 1 Timothy 4:14 " Do not neglect the gift that is in you, which was given to you by prophecy with the laying on of the hands of the eldership." Transference of Spirits is evident in Proverbs 13:20 which says, "He who walks with wise men will be wise." Likewise, if we walk with wise men their Spirits will be transferred on to us, we must therefore carefully select our associates. On the contrary, Proverbs 22:24-25 says, "Make no friendships with an angry Man, and with a furious man do no go, lest you learn his ways, and set a snare for your soul." Proverbs 14:7 says, "Go from the presence of a foolish man, when you do not perceive in him the lips of knowledge." Proverbs 4:14-15 says, "Do not enter the path of the wicked, and do not walk in the way of evil, avoid it, do not travel on it; turn away from it and pass on." We should be careful what Church we attend and who we listen to preaching on television and the radio Transference of Spirits can happen from receiving bad doctrine. 2 Cor. 11:3-4 says "But I fear, lest by any means, as the serpent beguiled Eve through his subtlety, so your minds should b corrupted from the simplicity that is in Christ. For if he that cometh preacheth another Jesus Whom we have not preached or if ye receive another spirit, which ye have not received, or another gospel, which ye have not accepted, ye might well bear with him. "If ye receive another spirit" well if since Paul is talking to the Corinthian, who are Christians, who already then have the Holy Spirit," Receiving another Spirit' can only apply to Evil Spirits especially in the context that the preaching is regarding "Another Jesus" and "another gospel" The Word of God says in 2 Cor. 6: 14-18 "Be ye not unequally yoked together with unbelievers: for what fellowship hath righteous with unrighteous? And what communion hath light with darkness? And what concord hath Christ with Belial? Or what part hath he that believeth with an infidel? And what agreement hath the temple of God with idols? For ye are the temple of the living God; as God hath said, I will dwell in them, and walk in them; and I will be their God, and they shall be my people. Wherefore come out from among them, and be ye separate, saith the Lord. And touch not the unclean thing: And I will receive you. And will be a Father unto you, and ye shall be my sons and daughters, saith the Lord almighty. Our major battles in life are not against people. They are against spirit forces. Jesus came into this earth to retrieve our lost dominion Jesus has told us that the world hates us, Jesus said if we were of the world that the world would love us. Jesus gave himself for our sins that he might deliver us, from this present Evil age, according to the will of God our Father. We have a Spirit that operates within the Spirit or heavenly realm, that Communicates with God, that Sees God, Hears God, Speaks to God, it is our Spirit that has been regenerated by The Holy Spirit of God. Transference of Spirits basically refers to Demonically Influenced Spirits that invade and intrude upon a person's spirit deceitfully assuming and invading upon the character, mannerisms, attitudes, desires and motives of a person. **God created our Spirits, It is the Spirit that gives life and at death the Spirit returns to God.** You have to learn to control your own spirit. Proverbs 25:28 says, "Whoever has no rule over his own Spirit is like a city broken down. Proverbs 16:32 says "He who is slow to anger is better than the mighty, and he who rules his spirit than he who takes a city. **Guard your ears, proverbs 20:19 says "he that goeth about as a talebearer revealeth secrets: therefore meddle not with him flattereth with his lips. Guard your tongue. Proverbs 10:19 says "In the multitude of words their wanteth not sin: but he that refraineth his lips is wise. Guard your eyes. Isaiah 32:3 says, "And the eyes of them that see shall not be dim, and the ears of them that hear shall hearken. Guard your affection.** Transference of Spirits is scriptural, you must control your own spirit, carefully select your associates, monitor friends of your children. There are Spiritual dangers in associating with those who have wrong spirits, guard your ears, your tongue, your eyes and guard your affections.

The Basis of Our Spirit Problems?

"No matter what I do to follow God, strange things happen to divert me from feeling that I am being blessed, like some others seem to be. It seems that I just continue to fall into the same sins and sinful behavior over and over again. I can't seem to get out of debt, sickness overtakes me, my children and spouse is sick, something happens to my business that is totally unforeseen, I just can't seem to figure out what is wrong!" These are good beginning questions, the answers lie in tracing the problems roots to one or more of the following reasons. Why Spirit-Filled believers are plagued by demons, demonic influence, evil spirits, unclean spirits, cursed living, family disasters and poverty. Many Spirit problems are the result of:

Sins
Iniquities
Transgressions
Not knowing God's WAYS or WILL
Not knowing, believing, or trusting God's character.
Not allowing Jesus Christ's Lordship in every area of life.
Not being willing to Hear as well as obey the voice of God.
Not loving God with your whole being.
Inheritance
    10. Wrong Choices
    11. Witchcraft

If with God's promised help you do no overcome the Spiritual problems and temptations of life, the sins of your self nature, or the wiles of the devil, you will be overcome by whatever you fail to overcome. To whatever you give the pre-eminence and priority to, will be the exact thing that will dominate your life.

The positive side is to put God first, leading you into "His" blessings. However if those priorities are out of God's will, they become idols that will erect a Spiritual Lordship within your Spirit gradually allowing Satan access to steal your freedom in Christ Jesus. Any problem a Spirit-filled believer cannot overcome by either prayer and fasting, repentance and forgiveness, the avid study of God's Word, or by spiritual discipline, is most likely due to an outside hindering force not natural to them. These characteristics show an evil spirit(s) in operation which is allowed power through the setting up of personal idols. Demonic Influence, Demons, Evil and Unclean Spirits deceive believers by placing within them unbelief that robs faith for prayer. Thus, deception will spiritually blind them to the true cause of their problems. Spiritual, outside hindrances causes true blindness in the Soul not allowing a person the ability to see the truth, not allowing them to see Jesus Christ as the cure for all their ailments, problems, oppressions, possessions, lack of fleshly control, and mental disturbances. They are overcome by Unbelief. Often this uncomfortable state escalates into anxiety or panic, causing the blinded deceived Believer to seek answers for their problems from the world instead of looking to God alone. These people now harassed in their spirits, souls and or bodies, may become extremely angry at God or others for "what they are going through' When these thoughts turn to unresolved bitterness and compulsive hatred, it will keep them from establishing a loving, open relationship with God in order to find true peace, meaning and purpose to their life. **All of this is traceable to Deceiving Spirits.** Satan of course, is pleased at his own helpfulness in the disastrous opportunity-wasted events in a believer's life and continues to ever bind blind and deceive his victim's for eventual destruction if possible. This root of bitterness will develop into hatred in the heart, hardening the heart of the believer and will then only move out of the life by repentance and the spiritual freedom that comes through Healing, Deliverance or Exorcism Ministry. There are about 1700 places in the Bible denoting "Deliver, deliverance, deliverer and the like" **Freedom from Evil Spirits and Demonic Influence Removes the supernatural parts of problems, then people are free enough to deal with the natural attachment of the Spirit, Soul and Fleshly Body.** "Ye shall diligently keep the commandments of the Lord your God, and his testimonies, and his statutes, which he hath commanded thee."And thou shalt do that which is right and good in the sight of the Lord: that it may be well with thee, and that thou mayest go in and possess the good land which the Lord Sware unto thy fathers. **To cast out all thine enemies from before thee, as the Lord hath spoken." Deuteronomy 6:17-19** And I will give peace in the land, and ye shall lie down, and none shall make you afraid: and I will rid evil beasts out of the land, neither shall the sword go through your land. And ye shall chase your enemies, and they shall fall before you by the sword .And five of you shall chase an hundred, and an hundred of you shall put ten thousand to flight: and your enemies shall fall before you by the sword. For I will have respect unto you, and make you fruitful, and multiply you, and establish my covenant with you. And ye shall eat old store, and bring forth the old because of the new. And I will set my tabernacle among you: and my soul shall not abhor you. And I will walk among you, and will be your God, and ye shall be my people.

I am the Lord your God, which brought you forth out of the land of Egypt, that ye should not be their bondmen; and I have broken the bands of your yoke, and made you go upright. Leviticus 26:6-13 stand fast therefore in the liberty wherewith Christ Hath made us free, and be not entangled again with the yoke of bondage. Galatians 5:1 The Lord redeemeth the Soul of his servants: and none of them that trust in him shall be desolate. Psalm 34:22 And Moses said unto the people, Fear ye not stand still, and see the salvation of the Lord…The Lord shall fight for you, and ye shall hold your peace. Exodus 14:13-14 and it shall come to pass, that Whosoever shall call on the name of the Lord shall be Delivered. Joel 2:32Jesus Healed all who came to "Him" of whatever problem, no matter how strong or violent the spirits were. In some places where "He" ministered, people's faith was stronger and "He" could do more. This meant that although the "gift of healing" within Jesus never changed or "lost power" the faith level of those with whom "Jesus" worked with was subject to their own allowed level of belief. In some places, the Son of God, God Himself, and a strong deliverer in the day of trouble to those who turn to "Him" was limited in ministry, by those that "He" came to bring healing and deliverance. "And Jesus went about all Galilee teaching in their synagogues, and preaching the gospel of the kingdom, and healing all manner of sickness."(Greek NOSOSINOSEO- to have a diseased appetite, to hanker after, (crave sickness) dote upon a malady, disability, disease, infirmity; clutching to self an evil thing.) …"and all manner of disease… (GREEK,MALAKIAN-softness or weakness to disease)"…among the people, And "His" fame went throughout all Syria and they brought unto "Him' custody of, or is a prisoner of physical or spiritual trouble), and torments…"(GREEK BASANISMOS/KAKOS-to maltreat, torture, make evil affected, vex, hurt, harm, pain, toil, toss)…"…those which were possessed with devils and those which were lunatic, and HE HEALED THEM ALL. Matt. 4:23-24 Now when the sun was setting, all they that had any sick with divers diseases, brought them unto "Him" and "He" laid "His" hands on EVERYONE OF THEM AND HEALED THEM and DEVILS ALSO *CAME OUT OF MANY,* crying and saying, Thou art Christ, the Son of God. And "He" rebuked them suffering them not to speak; for they KNEW that "He" was Christ. Lk.4:40-41, Mt 8:16, Mk 1:32-33 **Jesus promised in John 14:12 that "His" followers would do the same works and even greater works than those "He" did. The Devil knows this and believes the Word of God. Thou believest that there is one God; thou doest well: The devils also believe and tremble. James 2:19** Every since the fall of Adam there has been a spiritual battle going on for the possession of minds, soul's and spirits. With the ultimate loss being the very death of mankind. The word of God is very clear about the existence of Satan and his kingdom. Then Jesus was led up by The Spirit into the wilderness to be tempted by the devil. Matt. 4:1 and we read of Jesus' temptation that Jesus resisted and overcame Satan by the power of the Word of God. There are Spiritual powers under the authority of Satan and their only purpose is to torment, harass, buffet, and inflict sickness and disease upon the children of God, why? Because the children of God seem to realize their Spiritual image and likeness of God Our Father and creator. John 4:24 "God is Spirit, and those who worship Him must worship Him in Spirit and in truth." Genesis 1: 26-27 In the beginning God created…And God said, "Let us make man in our image, after our likeness and let them have dominion over the fish of the sea and over the fowl of the air, and over the cattle, **and over all he earth,** and over every creeping thing that creepeth upon the earth. Genesis 1: 27 So God created man in his own Image, in the image of God created he them. Because we are created in the image of God, it follows that, since God is Spirit-we are also Spirit. According to the Word of God, humans have three parts, Spirit, Soul and Body. 1 Thessalonians 5:23 Now may the God of peace Himself sanctify you completely; and may your whole Spirit, Soul and Body be preserved blameless at the coming of Our Lord Jesus Christ. Genesis 1:31 And God saw everything that he had made, and behold, It was very good. Genesis 2:7 And the Lord God formed man of the dust of the ground and breathed into his nostrils the breath of life and man became a living soul. Ecclesiastes 12:6-7 or ever the silver cord be loosed, or the golden bowl broken, or the pitcher be broken at the fountain or the wheel broken at the cistern. Then shall the dust return to the earth as it was: **And the Spirit shall return unto God who gave it. The Bible tells us that we are to do something with your Body, so your Body is not the real you, But something that you possess. Also the Bible teaches you that you are to renew your mind.** Romans 12:1-2 I beseech you therefore, brethren, by the mercies of God that you present your bodies a living sacrifice, holy, acceptable to God. Which is your reasonable service. And do not be conformed to this world, but be transformed by the renewing of your mind, that you may prove what is that good and acceptable and perfect will of God. **Nothing is said about your Spirit in this passage because your Spirit is the part of you that is born-again regenerated with new life of God "His Holy Spirit."** John 3:6-7, that which is born of the flesh is flesh, and that which is born of the Spirit is Spirit. "Do not marvel that I said to you "You must be born again." From this Scripture we see that when you are born-again, the part of you that is born-again is your Spirit-not your Soul or your Body. So, the real you, your Spirit, born-again, right with God, its creator and sender fills you with "His Life" The Holy Spirit, again, which Adam and Eve lost through sin. To say it clearly, you are a Spirit, you have a Soul (Your Mind, Will, Emotions and Intellect) and you live in a body. Your body is where the indwelling Spirit of God resides and the devil's desire is to pervert God's Holy Temple thereby defiling it. **You say, but I am a Christian, how can I have a Spirit other than The Holy Spirit of God? In the first place you must understand that you can have a demon, unclean, evil or familiar spirit, without being possessed by a demon.** Now there was a man in their synagogue with an unclean spirit…Mark 1:23, for John came neither eating nor drinking, and they say, "He has a demon" Matt. 11:18 "For a woman whose young daughter had an unclean spirit heard about him, and she came and fell at His feet. Mark 7:25 some people want to totally reject the thought that our bodies can simultaneously be inhabited both by the Holy Spirit and by a Demon, Evil or Unclean spirit. The King James version of the Bible and a few other versions, have translated *daimonzomai* as "demon possessed" whereas the word correctly means *"to act under the control of demons"* **Those who were thus afflicted expressed the mind and consciousness**

of the spirits that were afflicting them. Be it demons, evil or unclean spirits of bondage. Christians can be influenced, controlled and oppressed by Demonic forces who indwell them, but Demons cannot "Possess or Own" a Christian. On the other hand "Christians can and do "possess or own demons, by an act of their conscious or unconscious will." Demons, Demonic, Influence, Evil, Unclean and all Spirits of bondage indwelling within a Holy Spirit indwelt person are trespassing without Legal rights; **therefore they are subject to eviction in the authority of the Name of Jesus Christ, the one who** has redeemed such believers unto himself, by His Shed Blood on the Cross at Calvary. 1 Peter 1:18 **But you still want to know "How can a Demon, an Evil or Unclean Spirit dwells in a person who has the Holy Spirit within Him or Her? The answer is made clear by remembering that "Your Body Is a Temple of the Holy Spirit" 1 Corinthians 6; 19 The Temple in Jerusalem had three parts:** Outer Court, Holy Place and the Holy of **Holies.** The presence of God dwelt solely in The Holy of Holies. The three compartments in the Temple correspond to man's triune being: Body, Soul and Spirit. For the born-again Spirit-Filled Christian, the human spirit corresponds to the Holy of Holies, which is the dwelling place of the Holy Spirit. The Holy Spirit desires us to submit every area of our "Temple" to "His" control. Other Temple areas include the Mind, the Will, the Emotions, the Intellect (The Soul) and The Physical Body. Jesus found defilement in the Jerusalem Temple; however, the money changers and the merchants with doves and cattle were not in the Holy of Holies, but in the outer courts of the Temple. Jesus proceeded to "Cast-Out" all who defiled The Temple of God. **Defilement is not in the Spirit of the Christian but in the "Outer Courts" of the Mind, Heart, Will, Emotions, Intellect and the Physical Body.** There can be Defilement in the Outer Court, or the Body, while the presence of the Lord Jesus Christ remains in The Holy of Holies. **Jesus is highly displeased with such a condition. Jesus wants "His" Temple cleansed and every defiling Spirit, Cast out In His Name.**

The only "Spirit" influencing us is supposed to be
The "Spirit of God" what Evil Spirits know is that
What ever Spirit is InfluencingThe Mind, Heart, Will, or Soul
Of a person will Influence and or Control Everything about That Person If you compare most Spirit-Filled, Christians and Non-Christians today, you will find very little difference between them when it comes to the problems and difficulties that they are experiencing, both have sicknesses, diseases, fears, depression, marital problems, drinking, smoking, fornication and curses operating within their lives and bodies. The Word of God informs us that God created not only a material or physical world but also an invisible, spiritual or a heavenly realm consisting of Angels and other spiritual intelligence, such as Cherubim (Gen 3:24, Ezek 28:14-15) Seraphim (Isa. 6:1,6,) Living Creatures (Rev. 4-5 and other unnamed Hosts and Ministers of God. Psalms 84:1, Psalms 103:20-21, Psalms 148;2-5) The creations and existence of an invisible, Spiritual or Heavenly realm, as well as the visible, is illustrated again by The Apostle Paul in Colossians 1:16 "For by "Him" were all things created, that are in heaven, and that are in earth, visible and invisible, whether they be thrones or dominions, or principalities, or powers; all things were created by "Him" and for "Him" Psalms 148:2-5 says, Praise ye him, all his angels; Praise ye him, all his hosts; Praise ye him, sun and moon: praise him all ye stars of light. Praise him, ye heavens of heavens, and ye waters that be above the heavens. Let them praise the name of the Lord. For he commanded, and they were created. These invisible hosts, dwelling either in the presence of God or in heavenly regions in close proximity to the earth, are of two orders; **The Good and the Evil. The Word of God further divides these two orders into a hierarchy,** consisting of thrones, dominions, principalities, authorities, powers, world rulers, and Spiritual forces in the

heavenlies, Angels, Archangels, Princes, Cherubim, Seraphim and other Spiritual hosts. Some of the designations refer to Holy Angelic authority; others denote Evil Supernatural forces, while some may refer to either, depending on the context. Certainly, the powers of darkness and the Satanic confederacy are under consideration in such passages of the Word of God in Romans 8:38-39 which says, "For I am persuaded, that neither death, nor life, nor angels, nor principalities, nor powers, nor things present, nor things to come, nor height, nor depth, nor any other creature, shall be able to separate us from the love of God, which is in Christ Jesus. Matt. 12:24-26 says "But when the Pharisees heard it, they said, this fellow doth not cast out devils, but by Beelzebub the prince of the devils. And Jesus knew their thoughts, and said unto them, "Every kingdom divided against itself is brought to desolation; and every city or house divided against itself shall not stand: And if Satan cast out Satan, he is divided against himself; how shall then his kingdom stand? Eph. 6:12 says, "For we wrestle not against flesh and blood, but against principalities, against powers, against the rulers of the darkness of this world, against spiritual wickedness in high places." In Isaiah 14:13, Satan refers to the reality of his kingdom, saying" I will exalt my throne above the stars of God." Jesus Christ, Himself acknowledges its existence in Matt. 12:26 saying, "If Satan cast out Satan…how shall then his kingdom stand?" The Apostle Paul speaks of Satan as "The prince of the power of the air" (As the literal ruler of the authority of the air, or the regions in proximity to the earth) and as the god of this age. When Satan offered Jesus Christ the kingdoms of this world in return for his acknowledgement of himself as god. Jesus did not challenge his right to offer them. In fact, Jesus Christ "Himself" referred to Satan three times as "the ruler of this world" The Apostle John designates him as the head of this present world system. 1 John 5:19 says, "And we know that we are of God, and the whole world lieth in wickedness." Satan rules in world affairs and directs them from his throne in the heavenlies, men, women and governments, as well as educational, social, economic, financial, political and in some cases, religious institutions, are under the devils power to whatever extent they yield themselves to his influences. The present realm and sphere of Satan and his evil hierarchy of Spiritual wicked powers is not in hell. Matt. 25:41 says, "Then shall he say also unto them on the left hand, depart from me ye cursed, into ever lasting fire, prepared for the devil and his angels: Rev 12:7-9 says, And there was war in heaven: Michael and his angels fought against the dragon; and the dragon fought and his angels, and prevailed not: neither was their place found any more in heaven. And the great dragon was cast out, that old serpent, called the Devil, and Satan, which deceiveth the whole world: He was cast out into the earth, and his angels were cast out with him. The present realm and sphere of Satan's kingdom is in the heavenly realm and doubtless in close proximity to the earth. Eph. 2:2 says, "Wherein time past ye walked according to the course of this world according to the prince of the power of the air, the Spirit that now worketh in the children of disobedience. In Ephesians 6:12, it speaks of Spiritual wickedness in high places and it literally means "Heavens" or Heavenly regions or realms. The Word of God says that Satan walks up and down in the earth at will and has access to heaven's throne as the "accuser" of the brethren. In Job 1:7 it says, "And the Lord said unto Satan, whence comest thou? Then Satan answered the Lord, and said, from going to and fro in the earth, and from walking up and down in it." 1 Peter 5:8 says, "Be sober, be vigilant; because your adversary the devil, as a roaring lion, walketh about seeking whom he may devour." Satan has access to heaven's throne as the "Accuser of the Brethren" his present dominion is that of King and ruler over a vast kingdom and hierarchy of dark powers. As prince of the power of the air he rules over the godless. His designation in 2 Cor. 4:4 signifies his present Spiritual and Religious power and influence. In whom the god of this world hath blinded the minds of them which believe not, lest the light of the glorious gospel of Christ, who is the image of god, should shine unto them. If man does not call upon God for his needs, through the Name of Jesus Christ, there is only one other source of supernatural spiritual power that can answer him or her and that is Satanic, Evil and demonic. When a person calls upon these forbidden sources through ignorance or otherwise, the devil will accommodate him or her with help. But as a result of this opening to him and his influences, he will move in and begin to oppress him or her physically, mentally, spiritually, emotionally or financially. 1 John 3:8 says, "For this purpose the Son of God was manifested, that "He" might destroy the works of the devil. Jesus desires to help us. If our problems are not coming from outside of us than the problem has got to be coming from someplace else. By that I mean that sickness, diseases, fears, depression, marital problems, smoking, drinking, sexual problems and curses. **Can all have Spiritual Origins radiating from within or from the inside of a person.** In Mark 7: 21-23 Jesus said " For from within, (that is) out of the hearts of men, come base and wicked thoughts, sexual immorality, stealing, murder, adultery; coveting, (a greedy desire to have more, or something that belongs to someone else) dangerous and destructive wickedness, deceit; unrestrained (Indecent) conduct; and evil eye(envy), slander, (evil speaking, malicious misrepresentation, abusiveness) pride, (the sin of an uplifted heart against God and man) foolishness (folly, lack of sense, recklessness, thoughtlessness) All these evil (purposes and desires) come from within, and they make the man unclean and render him or her unholy. All of these are the names of Evil Spirits, Demons and Demonic Influence from Satan. Do you have a problem? Well, if the problem is being caused by Evil Spiritual demonic influences, guess where those Spirits are located? They are inside of your Physical Human Body, which houses your Soul. This is why Jesus said to us to; Cast the Demonic Spirits Out, In His Name.

You and I are Triune beings;

We have a Body and in that Body resides our Soul and our Spirit.

Our Bodies:

Demons, Demonic Influence, Evil, Unclean, Infirmity, Spirits of bondage, get into our bodies and cause us to have sicknesses, diseases and problems that torment and plague us. Do you or a family member have cancer? What about diabetes, high blood pressure, heart trouble, those are all demonically influenced and can be inherited.

Our Souls:

Our Souls consists of our Hearts, our Minds, our Wills and Our Emotions. The Evil Spirits, Demonic Influences, get into our souls or what is sometimes referred to as our Soulish realm and causes us to think, do and act in a way that we shouldn't do and wish we hadn't done. Do you have a bad temper? Are there mental problems or suicide in your family background? Do you have trouble with bad thoughts, lying, or suddenly your memory is going? Not always the case however those can all be manifestations of demonic influences in operation.

Our Spirits:

Evil Spirits, Demons and Demonic Influence cannot get into your Spirit: Because this is where Jesus and The Holy Spirit reside within your Temple or Body, The Holy of Holies, within each Spirit-Filled Christian, whose body has become The Temple of God here on earth.

Here is what you have to understand, Evil Spirits, Demons and Demonic Influence, can have your Spirit surrounded and this is where the internal war takes place, because you will be having trouble serving the Lord Jesus Christ, the way that the Word of God tells us to. You will have trouble reading the Bible, Praying, Studying and Fasting. This is how Christians can and do have Evil demonic influences operating within their lives. **Try this clasp your two hands together tightly interlocking your fingers squeezing them together as hard and as tight as you can. So that nothing can get into your palms, not even air. This is what Evil Spirits and Demonic Influences do to our Spirits, the place where Jesus and the Holy Spirit reside.** When you have prayed to know avail about a problem then there can be Evil Spirits, Demonic Influences involved within doing their jobs. Those Spirits have job assignments. They perform their jobs all day and all night long every day of the week with no breaks, any time off or vacation days. A lying demonic spirit or influence makes a person lie. A fear demonic spirit or influence makes a person afraid. A temper demonic influence or spirit makes a person have a bad temper and be angry and filled with rage. A suicide spirit or demonic influence makes a person want to kill themselves. A pain demonic influence or spirit causes a person to have pain and suffering. A poverty demonic influence or spirit will keep a person in lack and poor, never having enough or anything, and the list goes on and on. The Evil Spirits and Demonic Influences are old, experienced and they tend to become very familiar with their victims, therefore making them very good at their jobs.

So let's take a realistic look at where we are today, Children of God and we have all kinds and types of problems, sick in our bodies, sick in our minds, can't seem to serve God the way that we want to, don't even have enough money to give to the work of The Lord in missions, or in the offerings. Working every day with nothing left over for anything that you just want to have or would like to do for your families and, Yes, that's right, I am telling you that Evil Spirits, Demonic Influences and Demons can and are causing us these problems. Jesus said, in John

10:10 "That Satan has come to kill, steal, and destroy, But that "He" Jesus has come to give us life and life more abundantly. Jesus said in Luke 13:32 "I cast out devils, and I do cures, today and tomorrow, and the third day, I shall be perfected." **Let me ask you this question, Are you a believer?** Many believers in the Bible had Demons Influencing them or Evil Spirits, Paul said so, (He said that it was a messenger From Satan) Jesus told Peter" Get behind me, Satan" because the Evil Spirit or Demonic Influence had gotten into Peter. The woman who was a daughter of Abraham and bowed over all those years was a Believer. In Luke 13:16 Jesus, said"And ought not this woman, being a daughter of Abraham whom Satan hath bound, lo these eighteen years, to be loosed from this bond on the Sabbath day? Mary Magdalene was a Believer, and had demons, Evil Spirits cast out of her. In Mark 16:9 it says, "Now when Jesus was risen early the first day of the week, "He" appeared first to Mary Magdalene' out of whom "He" had cast seven devils. The Word of God goes on to say in Luke 8:2 "And certain women, which had been healed of Evil Spirits and infirmities, Mary called Magdalene, out of whom went seven devils." It is no wonder that so many people are suffering needlessly today. The Devil moved Casting out of demons from the Church about 300 years after Jesus rose from the dead. Being made free from Spiritual bondage is another blessing, a Miracle from God, a gift from God, a blessing to make our life down here within this earthly realm better. Just as Salvation is a Miracle a Blessing and an experience with God, being made free from Evil Spirits and Demonic Influences is a miraculous experience that only God can bring about. Jesus told the woman of Canaan, that Deliverance was the Children's bread. Jesus said in Matt. 15:26" Let the children first be filled: for it is not meet to take the Children's bread and cast it unto the dogs." However When Jesus heard her faith and this mother's love for her child, in desiring her child's freedom. Jesus said in Matt. 15:28" O woman great is thy faith; be it unto thee even as thou wilt: and her daughter was made whole from that very hour. In Mark 7:30 it says, "And when she was come to her house, she found the devil gone out, and her daughter laid upon the bed." So Christians, who has Evil Spirits or Demonic Influences? **Everyone has! "Demonic Influences or Evil Spirits are anything that controls, harasses, torments, plagues or drives you to do things that you know you shouldn't do, wish you hadn't done and can't stop doing."** I want to assure you of something Jesus Christ has already provided freedom and help; this was done at Calvary, through Jesus' shed blood, which is still flowing for us today.

Jesus can heal your insides, as well as your outsides and Jesus has already told us through "His" word that **"He" would come and heal us.** In Mark 9:39 Jesus, says that Casting Out Demons or Evil Spirits, Demonic Influences is a Miracle. **The first step is that you have to actually believe that you might be experiencing a Spirit Problem. And that if it is a spirit problem, it has to be coming from Evil Spirits, Demonic influences, Unclean, Infirmity, Spirits of Bondage. And you have got to accept the fact that if it is a Spirit Problem it is going to require a Spirit solution.**

You see if you do not believe, or cannot accept the possibility that you could possibly have an Evil Spirit, Demonic Influence, Unclean Spirits of bondage, tormenting, harassing, plaguing and working against you. Then you will never receive any help from God in this area. Why, because if you don't accept the fact that you possibly could have a Spiritual problem. That may have been brought on by Evil Spirits or Demonic Influences and someone tries to help you by Casting those Spirits and their Influences out, then those Spirits do not have to leave you and the problems will begin to intensify themselves. That is why you must humble yourself and say, "Well maybe I could have a Spirit problem, and if I have any Evil Spirits, or Demonic Influences operating in me than, I want them out, in the name of Jesus.

"Let me ask you this question? Why should you die, before your time?

Jesus came to set us free. Jesus came to destroy the works of the devil, in us, on us, around us and through us,

Or would you prefer that the Demonic Influences, or Evil Spirits that you don't think that you have continue to keep you and your loved ones in bondage?

Before you got saved you didn't believe that either, you had to submit to Jesus for your Salvation, well it's the same thing with your Spirit Freedom. You see Salvation and Deliverance go hand in hand. Jesus, said to you and I giving us instructions in Luke 10:19 'Behold, I have given you authority and power (Physical and mental strength and ability) to trample upon serpents and scorpions and over all the power that the enemy (possesses) and nothing shall in any way harm you. "Jesus told us in 2 Cor. 10:4 exactly what we have to use against the enemy and how spirit powerful they are against our spirit enemies. "For the weapons of our warfare are not physical (weapons of flesh and blood) but they are mighty before God, for the overthrow and destruction of Spirit Strongholds. Demonic Spirit influences or Evil Spirits in control (within) a person is anything that controls, harasses, torments, plagues, or drives you to do things that you know you shouldn't do wish you hadn't done and can't stop doing." We are called to war against all evil spirits (Ephesians 6:12). Only in Jesus Christ's power and authority can we drive them out of their positions of influence. Satan's works include sickness, inspiring false religion, strife and wars, creating poverty and oppression, leading people to torment and eternal hell. The goal of the Devil is to rob Spirit-Filled Believers of their inheritance in Christ.

Spirit Problems

As They Relate to

Spirit-Filled Believers

Whatever, we Spirit-filled people, do not overcome spiritually, we will be overcome by it spiritually. Whatever we give pre-eminence and priority to in our lives will be the exact thing that will dominate our live. If our priorities are out of God's will, those things will become idols in our lives that will erect a Spiritual Lordship within our Spirit. Any problem that we have as a Spirit-filled believer that cannot be overcome by either prayer, fasting, repentance, avid study of the Word of God, or by Spiritual discipline, then this situation is most likely due to an outside spiritual force not natural to us working from within or without. If with God's promised help we are not able to overcome the temptations of this world, the sins of our self-nature, or the wiles of the devil it is most likely that we have a spiritual problem. These characteristics reveal that an intruding spiritual influence is being allowed power to operate. Evil and Demonic influences, deceive Christian Believers by placing within us doubt and unbelief that will try to rob us of our faith. Bring into our Spirits an unbelief that robs and causes to bring doubt within us about God's ability to answer our specific prayer needs. Thus, this deception will spiritually blind us to the true cause and symptoms of our problems. Spiritual outside hindrances can cause true blindness within the human spirit causing us not to be able to see Jesus Christ as the real cure for all of our ailments, problems, Oppressions, Possessions, lack of fleshly control and mental, physical, emotional, financial and spiritual problems.

Outside Spiritual obstacles and forces that can cause us to become spiritually blinded and fearful by doubt and unbelief. Many times this uncomfortable spiritual state escalates into anxiety or panic self-defeatism or apostasy, which is a lack of faith, thus causing us to seek answers from outside sources instead of looking to God. This is what causes us to become harassed and heavy within our Spirits. It can and many times does cause us to become extremely angry at God. And at others, that The Lord Jesus is using to bring the much needed help and freedom so desperately needed at this time. What we are going through when these thoughts turn into unresolved issues, many times resulting in bitterness and compulsive hatred will keep us from establishing a loving open relationship with God and others. All of this is traceable to a Spiritual Problem with the root cause of the problem being Evil, Unclean, Familiar, and Demon Spirits with Spirit Demonic influences. Satan is of course pleased at his own helpfulness in the situation, because of course he has everyone convinced that he has nothing to do with any of it. He goes on continuing to ever blind his victims for eventual destruction if possible. One of the names of our Spiritual enemy is Beelzebub which was the god of the flies. Let's take a comparative look at the annoying nature of files with a comparative look at the annoying nature of flies with a comparative eye on the annoyances of Demonic Influence:

*Flies are carriers of various diseases, some of which are deadly. (Demonic influence also causes various diseases or infirmities to our minds, bodies and souls.)

*Flies fly in the air. (Satan is the prince of the powers of the air)

*Flies show up right before a rain or change in the weather (Demonic influence appears to attack right at the point God is making a change in our lives.

*Flies distract us and harass us. (Demonic influences main purpose is to distract and harass us)

*Flies infect open wounds. (Demonic influence does the same thing with emotional wounds causing them to spread)

*Flies are attracted to that which is spoiled and refuse (Demonic influence pulls us toward perversion, lust and that which is unclean.)

*Flies are attracted to and spoil our food. (Demonic influences come to kill, steal, and destroy)

*Flies often bring the fear of harm. (Demonic influence uses fear as their greatest weapon against us)

*Flies bite us inflicting pain and sometimes causing bodily harm (Demonic influences may also bite s and cause us great physical torment.)

*Flies sometimes eat and kill plants intended for our food. (Satan is described as the devourer.)

*Flies find the smallest of openings and enter into our houses. (Demonic influences also find the smallest openings and enter into us.

*Flies often just buzz around us. (Satan is described as a roaring lion)

The only cure for a Spiritual problem is that the spiritual part of the problem must be discerned. And we must receive spiritual healing, deliverance and exorcism removing the spiritual part so that, than through further ministry the natural attachment of the Soul and the Flesh can receive what it needs in order for us to be made whole and complete, lacking nothing.

Listed below are five areas that definitely can bring about

Spiritual problems, In the Life of a Sprit-Filled Believer:

- Not knowing God's will or way
- Not knowing, believing or trusting God's character.
- Not allowing Jesus Christ's lordship in every area of our lives.
- Not being willing to hear as well as obey the voice of instruction from God.
- Not loving God, with our Hearts, Minds, Souls and Bodies.

Every Spiritual problem is the result of Evil Spirits, Unclean and Familiar Spirits, Demons and Demonic Spirit Influence. However, we can also be experiencing spiritual bondage because of the fact that we have overlooked or denied the reality of Spirit Influences at work in the world. Our inheritance in Jesus Christ, through The Word of God is our basis for believing and knowing that Peace of Mind and Spiritual Good health of Spirit, Soul and Body is ours.

Jesus Calls Casting Out Devils (Spirits) A Miracle

"And John answered him, saying, Master, we saw one casting out Devils in Thy Name, and he followeth not us: and we forbade him, because he followeth not us. (Verse 39) But Jesus said, forbid him not; for there is no man **Which Shall Do a Miracle In my name, That can lightly speak evil of me."** Mark 9:38-39. **Jesus himself called Casting Out Devils, A Miracle.** When Jesus gave the great commission, "He" told his followers to do more than just preach the Word of God, Jesus said, in Matthew 10:7-8, "And as ye go, preach…Heal the Sick…Cast Out Devils. Preaching the Word of God, (Preaching Jesus) shows people that it is possible to be free, but casting The Devils out of those people makes them free indeed. You see Jesus himself did more than just Preach, the Word of God and Jesus was and is The Word of God, made flesh. Jesus, set the captives free and Jesus cast out devils. When Phillip went to Samaria, he did more than just preach Jesus to the people. Phillip the Evangelist preached Jesus Healed the sick and cast out Evil, Unclean, Familiar, and Demonic Spirits. Exhibiting The Miracle of Deliverance. In Acts 2:21, it says

"And it shall come to pass, that whosoever Shall call on the name of the Lord, shall be saved." Joel 2:32 says, **and it shall come to pass, that Whosoever shall call on the Name of the Lord shall be Delivered:** For in mount Zion and in Jerusalem shall be Deliverance, as The Lord hath said, **and**

In The Remnant whom The Lord Shall Call. Jesus

came into this world, as God, Himself, manifested in the flesh, and appeared in human form, as a Living Miracle. Now look at this, If you can accept: The Miracle of Jesus' Miraculous Birth, The Miracle of Jesus' spinelessness, The Miracle of Jesus' Crucifixion, The Miracle of Jesus' Death, The Miracle of Jesus' Burial and The Miracle of Jesus' Glorious Resurrection! Then you should be able to believe that any other miracle through Jesus is possible and you should be able to believe, **that Jesus is, Jesus of the Miraculous! You should be able to believe that Jesus Is the Miraculous resurrected Son of God, and you should be able to Believe that Jesus, is The Jesus of Miracles.** A Miracle is a supernatural act of God that appears difficult to explain or account for, by the laws of nature or man. The Miracle of Deliverance is a supernatural act of God rescuing a person from bondage, from danger, from torment or evil. The Miracle of Deliverance is a supernatural delivering that takes place by God. A Deliverance that moves or transports, circumstances, situations, individuals and Spirits to there proper place and that is away from the Child of God. The Miracle of Deliverance is a supernatural act of God that sets individuals free, depending upon and in accordance with their personal area of need, and according to God's plan for their life. Another name for Miracle, In the Word of God is Wonder: A wonder is something that causes awe, surprise, or admiration, something that causes one to wonder? Be puzzled, astounded or to marvel at. Another name for miracle in The Word of God is a sign: A sign is an indicator, or something that suggests the presence or existence of a fact, condition, or quality. An act or gesture used to convey an idea, a desire, information or a command. Acts 2:19 "And I will shew Wonders (Miracle) in heaven above and Signs, (Miracles) in earth beneath; blood and fire and vapour of smoke." Acts 2:21"And it shall come to pass, that whosoever shall call on the Name of The Lord, shall be saved." The out pouring of the Holy Ghost the accompanying Miracles (Signs), The Power and the Blessings of The Holy Ghost are for every Believer to have and experience through out the Church age. From Jesus' baptism on, The Holy spirit was fully Up-on **Him** as Christ, the anointed one, anointed by the Holy Ghost, now at the right hand of God. Jesus, ever lives to pour forth, the same Spirit, upon those who believe in him. It was prophesied in Isa. 61: **The Spirit of The Lord God is up-on me, because the Lord hath anointed me to preach good tidings unto the meek, He hath anointed me to preach good tidings unto the meek, He hath sent me to bind up the Broken-hearted. To proclaim liberty to the captives and the opening of the prison to them that are bound. To proclaim the acceptable year of the Lord, and the day of vengeance of our God; to comfort all that mourn. To appoint unto them that mourn in Zion, to give unto them beauty for ashes, the oil of joy for mourning, the garment of praise for the Spirit of heaviness; that they might be called trees of righteousness, the planting of the Lord, that He might be glorified.** This description of Jesus and His anointing relates to His mission or ministry. When Jesus began His ministry, Jesus quoted these verses, and applied them to Himself. In Luke 4:18, Jesus said, "The Spirit of the Lord is Up-on me, because he hath anointed me to **Preach the gospel to the poor; he hath sent me to heal the broken-hearted, to preach deliverance to the captives, and** recovering of sight to the blind, to set at liberty, them that are bruised." Jesus said, in John 4:48 "Then said Jesus unto him, except ye see signs (Miracles) and Wonders, ye will not believe." **In the book of Psalms, 37:39-40, it says, "But salvation of the righteous is of the Lord: he is their strength, in the time of trouble. And the Lord shall help them and Deliver them from the wicked, and save them, because they trust in him."** In the Word of God it tells us the King Darius wrote a decree, after God had supernaturally delivered Daniel from the lions den. God moved supernaturally in the Lions den for Daniel to deliver him. In Daniel 6:25-27, it says, "I make a decree, that in every dominion of my kingdom men tremble and fear before the God of Daniel: For He is the living God, and steadfast, forever, and His kingdom that which shall not be destroyed and his dominion shall be even unto the end. (Verse 27) **He Delivereth and Rescueth, and He worketh Signs and Wonders in heaven and in earth, who hath Delivered Daniel from the power of the lions.** Perhaps, when the King was preparing this decree; He had heard of God's deliverance of Daniel's three friends from the fiery furnace. In Daniel 3:19-30, Shadrach, Meshach, and Abednego, after they had refused to commit, The Sin of Idolatry, they said to King Nebuchadnezzar, that we will not serve thy god, nor worship the golden image which thou hast set-up. We all know what the three Hebrew boys told the King concerning, god's ability and power to deliver, they said," **If it be so, our God whom we serve is able to Deliver us, from the burning fiery furnace. And He will Deliver us, out of thine hand O King."** And you and I know the rest of the story. The counselor told the King, when the King asked about those three Hebrews, (verse 25) He answered and said, **Lo, I see four men loose, walking in the midst of the fire, and they have no hurt and the form of the fourth is like the Son of Man.** What he saw was a form, not a natural form but a supernatural form, a supernatural being in the form of The Son of god. Psalms 18:50 says, "Great Deliverance giveth he to his King; and showeth mercy to his anointed, to David and to His seed forever mine." Here you must begin to see the whole picture of God's delivering power. **God Delivered Noah and his family from the flood by the ark in Gen. 6; 8. God Delivered Lot and His family from the fiery destruction of Sodom and Gomorrah in** Gen.16:29, **God Delivered the whole nation of Israel, from Egyptian slavery through the exodus, preserving them by supernatural miraculous feedings in the wilderness in** Exodus 12; 17. **God Delivered David and His Army from capture by King Saul's Army on many occasions in** 1 Sam. 23; **God Delivered the Prophet Elijah, when he became fearful of Jezebel, running for his very life, God fed him by the ravens in the wilderness in** 1 Kings 17:2-6. Jesus said, for you and me to pray for Deliverance. When Jesus' disciples asked him how to pray in Matt. 6:9-13, Jesus says, in verse 9 "After this manner therefore pray ye, (verse 13) And lead us not into temptation **But Deliver us, from Evil"** In Acts Chapter 10:38 it says, "How God anointed Jesus of Nazareth with the Holy Ghost and with Power: Who went about doing good, and Healing all that were **Oppressed of the Devil for God was with Him.** In the many Miracles of Deliverance, that I have outlined here. Lies not so much in the Miraculous Supernatural power of God, that was displayed, but in the significance attached to them all and that is this. **Almighty God had a plan of Deliverance, already laid out for each of them, that loved him and trusted him.**

Almighty God had a plan of Deliverance already laid out for each of them that believed in Him. And god had a miraculous plan of Deliverance, Already laid out for those who could believe, stand and receive, their Deliverance, through God's plan and not their own plan, they submitted to God's plan by their Faith and Actions. In each of those Deliverance's God, Delivered them through Circumstances; God Delivered Daniel in the lions den. God Delivered, Shadrach, Meshach and Abednego, in the fire. God Delivered Noah, off of the flooded earth, into the ark, before the flood, shut in and protected by God, almighty, and his deliverance did not stop there. Noah was Delivered during the flood. God, Delivered Lot and his family, before the destruction, (however) his wife lost her deliverance, when a Worldly Spirit caused her to look back. God Delivered the nation of Israel, in the whole of their slavery. God Delivered David and his army again and again. God Delivered the prophet Elijah, even after a Spirit of fear had entered into him. And God sent his Son Jesus, into the world that we might be Saved, Healed and Delivered, **Jesus came into the world, as God himself, manifested in the flesh, and appeared as a Living Miracle in human spirit form at** the same time. And if you can accept the Miracle of Jesus' Birth, The Miracle of Jesus' Sinlessness, The Miracle of Jesus' Crucifixion, The Miracle of Jesus' Resurrection, Then you should be able to Believe that Jesus is Alive, Today and that any other Miracle through Jesus Is Possible. That Jesus is the Jesus of the Miraculous, made wholly of the Miraculous, The Resurrected Son of God. A Miracle "Himself" Given to us by The One True God of the Miraculous God, The Father and Operating by The Power of The Holy Spirit. **In Jesus' Earthly Ministry, Jesus did not Heal, Save and Deliver every sick person, every time. However Jesus did not refuse any who sought his help. Jesus passed by a great multitude and selected only one for healing** In John 5:3-6 it says, "In these lay a great multitude of impotent folk, of blind, halt, withered, waiting for the moving of the water. (Verse 5) And a certain man was there which had an infirmity thirty and eight years. When Jesus saw him lie, and knew that he had been now a long time in that case, he saith unto him, **Wilt thou be made whole? (The Jesus of the Miraculous) healed that man and delivered him form 38 years of Oppression, Misery, Pain, Physical and mental anguish. Delivered him from 38 years of anxiety. The Word of God says in (verse 6) "Jesus knew that he had been now a long time in that case." The Word of God says, "He was made whole." Jesus, Miracles symbolize His power through god to meet Spiritual, Physical and Mental needs. They are a testimony of His being, The Son of God, The second person of the Holy Trinity, Jesus Christ, fully God and fully man.** (Both Spiritual man and Natural man, at the same time and empowered by, The Holy Spirit of God) Jesus had then and Jesus has now a deep and unceasing compassion for those afflicted with Spiritual, Physical and Mental distress and Diseases. Jesus said, in Matt. 8:7, "I will come and heal him" In Luke 13:10-18, A Woman was in the Church, who had been crippled by a spirit for 18 years, The Word of God says that she was bowed together.

She had a Spiritual problem with a Demonic origin. As soon as Jesus Delivered her, the first thing that happened was that the physical problem was cured. This woman had been in bondage (verses 12 and 13) "And when Jesus saw her, he called her to himself, and said unto her, Woman thou Art loosed from thin infirmity." (Verse 13) And he laid his hands on her; and immediately she was made straight and glorified God." **Think about this, this woman was in the Church (synagogue) On the Sabbath Day, and had been in the Church on the Sabbath days for 18 years bound.** Isaiah 53:4-4 says, "Surely, he hath borne our Grief's, and carried our sorrows: yet we did esteem him stricken, smitten of God, and afflicted (verse5) But He was wounded for our transgressions, he was bruised for our iniquities, the chastisement of our peace was upon him; and with "His" stripes We are healed. Jesus has borne our griefs, Jesus has borne, both the physical and the mental griefs along with our spiritual griefs. Jesus has endured, just as it was prophesied. Jesus endured at the Cross on Calvary, endured that we might be Delivered. Delivered from our sins, Delivered from our sicknesses. Delivered from our Diseases, Just as Jesus bore our sins, Jesus also Delivered us. Jesus taking our grief, Jesus taking our sorrow, Jesus taking our anguish, Jesus taking our pains away, Jesus taking our sorrow, Jesus taking our anguish, Jesus taking our pains away, Jesus taking what was rightfully ours lifting them out of us up-on Himself. Jesus carried them then and Jesus carries them now! Today! Jesus was crucified, because we have sinned and are guilty before God. Jesus as our substitute took the punishment due us and paid the penalty for our sins. Therefore, through Jesus, we are forgiven, through Jesus, we have peace with God. 1 John 3:8 says, "For this purpose The Son of God was manifested, that he might destroy the works of the devil." Jesus did not highly esteem, the faith produced by "His Miracles. The Pharisees, wanted to see a sign, A Miracle, tempting Jesus, in Mark 8:11-12, it says…There shall no sign be given unto this generation. But this is not for us believers. Our first desire should not be for a Miracle or a Sign or even Deliverance which is a Miracle. It should not be coming to Jesus for something, out first desire should be to come to Jesus to know Jesus. To love Jesus, to be in God's perfect will. I want to share something with you that prayerfully will forever be the truth. Jesus, can and Jesus will, Deliver you and Heal you. Because God loves you, and it is the Will of God for you to be Saved, Healed and Delivered. Jesus' wonderful healings and deliverances reveal mans tremendous need and Jesus' miracles bring to light the ruin caused by sin and Jesus' miracles bring to light God's power and will to repair that damage. To heal broken-hearts, and to set-the captives free. Jesus can and Jesus will heal and deliver by remote control. Sometimes however you have to reach up and touch Jesus for your healing and deliverance. Sometimes Jesus, heals and delivers on the faith of others, sometimes Jesus heals and deliver without any faith at all. Then again sometimes healing and deliverance is dependent upon your faith. I want to make one thing very clear to you, and that is. If you are full of doubt and unbelief, you don't even have to worry about receiving anything from Jesus. Matt. 13:58 says, "And he (Jesus) did not many mighty works there because of their unbelief." Mark 6:5-6 says, "And he (Jesus) did not many mighty works there because of their unbelief." Mark 6:5-6 says, "And He (Jesus) could there do not mighty work, save that He (Jesus) laid His hands upon a few sick folk and He (Jesus) healed them." (Verse 6) "And He (Jesus) marveled because of their unbelief. And he went round about the villages, teaching." You must believe in Jesus and your belief, must come from your heart. According to Matt. 9:22 it says, If you believe right now your faith working through belief in Jesus, If you believe In Jesus today, according to your faith be it done unto you. If you believe in Jesus today, do not be afraid, only believe, if you believe in Jesus today, your faith in Jesus will insure your Healing Deliverance Miracle. If you Believe Jesus Today, Everything is possible to him who believes, If you Believe Jesus Today. The Miracle of Deliverance can be a reality of Jesus for you. If you can Believe Jesus Today Great is your faith. If you Believe Jesus Today, your prayer is effective through Jesus. If you Believe Jesus Today, You can ask and receive through Jesus, The wonderful Miracle of Deliverance. Jesus Delivering you setting you free, allowing you to operate in your God given mind. Jesus, Delivering you from 2lack, poverty and depravation, rebuking the devourer from your finances. Jesus Delivering Mothers from loss, grief and sorrow. Jesus will Deliver Sons, Daughters, Mothers, Fathers, Grandchildren, whole families. Jesus, loosing you and restoring you. Jesus bringing new life, Delivering from Spiritual and Natural Bondage and Blindness giving you new sight to old circumstance and situations, Jesus, Delivering from Spiritual Death, Delivering you into Resurrection life and power. Jesus giving you a Miracle of Deliverance, Life and that more Abundantly. Giving you, and yours, a Miracle of Deliverance.

The Spirits are Subject Unto You!

Jesus was equipped for His earthly ministry, according to the Word of God…being baptized in the Jordan River by, John the Baptist. Matt. 3:16 "And Jesus, when He was baptized, went up straightway out of the water: and, lo, the heavens were opened unto Him, and He saw The Spirit of God descending like a dove and lighting upon him. Chapter 4 verse 1 says, "Then was Jesus led up of the Spirit, **(The Holy Spirit led Jesus)** into the wilderness to be tempted of the devil. **Being full of the Holy Spirit, Jesus was able to face Satan and to resist his temptation. Jesus began His earthly ministry by preaching to the people** "Repent: for the Kingdom of Heaven is at hand." **Jesus began His ministry** in the Synagogue or the Church by Ministering (reading) Out of the Word of God. **"The Spirit of the Lord is upon me,** because he hath anointed me to preach the gospel to the poor; he hath sent me to heal the broken-hearted, to preach deliverance to the captives, and recovering of sight to the blind, to set at liberty them that are bruised. To preach the acceptable year of the Lord." Luke 4:18. **Then Jesus began to operate in His Ministry, Spiritually, having been endued with power from on high, from His Father God and Our Father. Power (supernaturally) from the Holy Spirit, Jesus, turned water into wine. Healed an official's son at Capernaum. Cast out a demon in Capernaum. Jesus healed Peter's Mother-in-law. Jesus healed a leper. Jesus caused some frustrated fishermen to catch a haul of fish. Jesus healed a paralytic. Jesus healed a crippled man. Jesus healed a hand that had shriveled up. Jesus healed a centurion's servant. Jesus raised a widow's son from the dead. Jesus, cast out a demon. Jesus stilled a storm. Jesus cast out demons in Gadara, Jesus healed a woman's bleeding and raised Jairus' daughter from the dead. Jesus healed two blind-men. Jesus healed a mute man. Jesus fed five-thousand people. Jesus walked on water. Jesus healed a Canaanite woman's daughter. Jesus fed another four thousand people. Jesus healed a deaf man. Jesus healed a blind man at Bethsaida. Jesus cast demons out of a boy. Jesus provided the temple tax for Peter and Himself from a fish's mouth. Jesus healed ten lepers. Jesus healed a man born blind. Jesus raised**

Lazarus from the dead. Jesus healed a crippled woman. Jesus healed a man with dropsy. Jesus healed two blind men. Jesus spoke a word and a fig tree died. Then Jesus died and was resurrected, through the power of the Holy Spirit. After Jesus' resurrection, Jesus ascended into heaven and sat down at the right hand of His Father as co-ruler of God's Kingdom. In this exalted position Jesus received the Holy Spirit from His Father and sent Him forth upon His people at Pentecost. **This out pouring testifies to the continual presence and the authority of Jesus this day. The Holy Spirit came to this earth to dwell within Believers on the day of Pentecost filling them with His Spirit.** "And when the day of Pentecost was fully come they were all with one accord in one place. And suddenly there came a sound from heaven as of a rushing mighty wind, and it filled all the house where they were sitting. And there appeared unto them cloven tongues like as of fire, and it sat upon each of them **and they were all filled with the Holy Ghost (A Spiritual Experience) and began to speak with other tongues, as The Spirit gave them utterance.** The Holy Spirit is now present in everyone who has asked Him to come and dwell within them, trusting Jesus as Savior and Lord. Because The Holy Spirit is indwelling within us, we have immediately become a Spirit human being having been born-again. Baptized into the Spirit Kingdom of God. A Spirit-filled person by the faith of God. Thus having become a child of God. Entitled to have and maintain an intimate loving relationship with God, Our Father, Jesus the Son and God the Holy Spirit. **Due to our Spiritual relationship with God, we are called to surrender ourselves to the Holy Spirit and as we make this surrender. The power of The Holy Spirit is released within us. Spiritually Transforming us from within. A Transformation that empowers us from within. God almighty empowers us with the same power that He empowered our Lord and Savior Jesus Christ.** Our Transformation is an inner transformation. A Transformation of our natural heart into a Spirit heart, a heart in union and in communion with God. A Spirit heart that begins to grow within the grace of God. A Spirit Transformation taking place within our understanding as God wants us to understand. A Spirit Transformation that begins to teach us to rely on God Our Father. A Spirit Transformation that teaches us to trust and have faith in God. A Spirit Transformation that restores us to a place with God. **A Spirit Transformation takes place within The Kingdom of God that we human spirits have never known before and could not ever have known within this natural, physical or material world. (Because this place was lost by Eve and Adam during the fall) A place that our Spirits had with God in heaven before the foundations of the earth. A Spirit Transformation takes place that is based upon Spirit Intimacy (A love relationship with God) that was lost and now found and has its residency within the heart of each Spirit-filled person.** A Spirit Transformation bringing about a knowing within the Spirit heart of the Spirit-Filled-person that He or She is safe within God's Love. Because The Spirit-Filled-person that dwells in God's love has the assurance of the reality of God. **Jesus says, I will manifest myself to him The Spirit-Filled person.** "Manifest means to make plain so Jesus says to the Spirit-Filled person "I will make myself real to you." Jesus promises to reveal himself to make "Himself" real to any Believer who will keep his commandments and Matt. 22:37-38 says, "Jesus said unto him, Thou shalt love the Lord thy God, with all thy heart, and with all thy soul, and with all thy mind. This is the first and great commandment. And the second is like unto it, Thou shalt love thy neighbor as thyself." Spirit-Filled Persons are called to know the real presence and reality of God. Which is the Love of God (Because God is Love). And knowing this Spirit Love of God. We become spirit motivated by this love of God to do those spirit things that are fruitful to God and bring him glory. This Spirit Transformation takes place within our hearts. Begins to cause us to love the things that God loves and to hate the things that God hates. This spirit transformation that takes place within us begins to cause us to take on the mind of Jesus Christ. This spirit transformation that is taking place within us causes us to want to be led by the resident Spirit of God that is within us, The Holy Spirit. We begin to want to know more about God and the more we hunger and thirst for God. The more we then begin to be transformed within our Souls and Bodies into the image and likeness of God spiritually. Now we have begun to become a threat to the Kingdom of Satan. And if you the Spirit-Filled Person has not yet been taught about the spirit battle which is taking place within you, then you my friend are functioning through a spiritual disadvantage. Because the warfare is a spirit battle, that will have natural and material manifestations. This spirit battle will be fought using your own personal spirit problems that came (or that are being exposed) to you as you, the Spirit-filled person becomes closer to God. And the battle will begin to escalate as you the Spirit-filled believer becomes closer to God. And the battle will begin to escalate as you the Spirit-filled person during this transformation process begins to be renewed in the renewing of your own mind taking on the mind of Christ Jesus. As you the Spirit-filled person begins to crucify your own flesh becoming dead to sin. And as you the Spirit-Filled Person begins to understand and accept your authority and power that is resident within you. (Spirit) through the fruits and the gifts of the Holy Spirit. Satan, will then begin to target you specifically just like he did Jesus in the wilderness, because he understands that God's final victory has already been won. Satan understands that he has been judged and sentenced and that very soon that sentence will be carried out. That Jesus' promise of total transformation will be fully realized. Satan understands better than you do that as a Spirit-filled person, filled with the Spirit of God, that you have been called to help Usher in God's Kingdom here on earth. That you have been raised up within the Spirit realm and will be instrumental in dislodging all of his Spirit powers and forces of hell. You see Satan understands that Spiritually **You are the Stronger Spirit; you have The Spirit of God residing within you. The Spirit of God that is over all that is, over all that exists, over all that ever will exist Spiritually and Naturally within the earth, above the earth and under the earth. You the Spirit-Filled have to begin to take Spirit responsibility and understand that your Spirit Man or Woman has been resurrected with the resurrection life of Jesus with Power over all the power of the Enemy.** Satan knows that as long as he can secretly hide a spirit hindrance, a spirit crippler or a spirit stronghold within your soul or body that you cannot be as effective within the Kingdom of God as you should be. So he inflicts all sorts of Spirit distresses and sicknesses within the inside of the Spirit-Filled person, thinking that you will never look in the most obvious place of all. While working his plan to kill us, steal from us and destroy us with different harassment's and plagues. And Satan does all of this dirty work from within the spirit realm operating Spirits within the life of the Spirit-filled person. Then Satan has us looking all over the world for the solutions and answers to the things that he is doing or has done, looking everywhere accept within the Spirit realm and looking at everything and everybody, except himself, Satan as the source of the problems.**"Spirit-filled people rise up and get rid of everything that is robbing you from within your Spirit, Soul and Body" And the God of peace will crush Satan under your feet shortly Romans 16:20 Spirit-filled people Rise up and begin to act like the victor that Jesus has enabled us to be. There is through faith, a heavenly or spiritual realm that enables us to become more spirit alive than we could ever be on our own. Spirit-filled people begin taking on an attitude with your spirit of a spiritual conqueror. "For I am persuaded that neither death, nor life, nor angels, nor principalities, nor powers, nor things present, nor things to come, nor height nor depth, nor any other created thing**

shall be able to separate us from the love of God which is in Christ Jesus Our Lord and Savior. Romans 8:38, 39 Spirit-filled people arise. Show Satan the resident wisdom, power and the strength of God that is within you. The power of the Holy Spirit that came through Jesus. Our Lord and Savior Jesus, who came to this earth in demonstration of the defeat of Satan. Jesus the omnipotent Son of the living God fully God and fully man empowered by the Holy Spirit. Jesus has dominion over all principalities, thrones, dominions and powers, on earth, under the earth and in heaven. Jesus who created principalities, thrones, dominions and Satan." For by him were all things created that are in heaven, and that are in earth, visible and invisible, whether they be thrones, or dominions, or principalities, or powers: all things were created by him, and for him and he is before all things, and by him all things consist." Colossians 1:16-17 Jesus, the Logos, Word of God, who was Satan's master when he came to this earth, who came so that you and I, as Spirit-filled people would have an example through the written Word of God. And a demonstration of God's Spiritual design for our lives as they relate to Satan. By Spiritual force, which was Jesus' complete power spiritually and naturally over Satan. And by design in the divine plan of God: providing for us, every Spirit-filled person a picture an illustration, of the resident spiritual abilities within us as the righteousness of God. To have power over all the power of the enemy and that nothing shall by any means harm us. It says in 2 Cor. 2:11 "Lest Satan should get an advantage of us: for we are not ignorant of Satan's devices." Begin to command Satan and his hosts out of any areas of your life. Ask, Jesus to show you if what is written in this books is the truth or not? If God tells you that it is the truth then you should ask God, to deliver you from any and all areas within the spirit realm that Satan may have hidden or deceptive strongholds in place within your Soul or body. Ask God to open your spiritual eyes and ears, so that you can see and hear spiritually from him as he reveals things to you from within "His heavenly realm" and then you take spiritual responsibility for your part of the prophetic vision (which is a spiritual vision) of God and do what ever the Lord Jesus instructs you to do in helping usher in "His" Kingdom here on earth. Cleanse your spiritual temple, which is the home of the indwelling Spirit of God. Remember that you have been chosen and appointed to bear fruit for God. Remember that you are God's workmanship and that you can approach God with confidence. Knowing that you can do all things through Christ Jesus, who strengthens you both Spirit and Naturally. Always keep in mind that you are united with God, and that you are one with "Him in Spirit." **You have been established, Anointed and sealed by God, Spirit-filled people.** Jesus said in Matt. 12:28-29 "But if I cast out devils by the Spirit of God, then the Kingdom of God is come unto you. Or else, how can one enter into a strong man's house and spoil his goods, except he first bind the strong man? And then he will spoil his house. Jesus said in Matt. 12:43-45 "When the unclean spirit is gone out of a man, he walketh through dry places, seeking rest, and findeth none. Then he saith, I will return into my house from whence I came out; and when he is come, he findeth it empty, swept and garnished. Then goeth he, and taketh with himself seven other spirits more wicked than himself, and they enter in and dwell there: and the last state of that man is worse than the first. Even so shall it be also unto this wicked generation." Jesus said, in Matt. 15:18 "But those things which proceed out of the mouth come froth from the heart; and they defile the man." In Matt. 10: it says" And when he had called unto him his twelve disciples, he gave them power, against unclean spirits, to cast them out and to heal all manner of sickness and all manner of disease…Jesus said, And as ye go, preach, saying the Kingdom of heaven is at hand. Heal the sick, cleanse the lepers, raise the dead, cast out devils; freely ye have received, freely give…For it is not ye that speak, but the Spirit of your Father which speaketh in you." Jesus said in Luke 9:25 "For what is a man advantaged, if he gain the whole world, and lose himself, or be cast away." In Luke 10:1 it says, "After these things the Lord appointed other seventy also, and sent them two and two before his face into every city and place, whither he himself would come." And the seventy returned again with joy, saying Lord, even the devils are subject unto us through thy name. And he said unto them, I beheld Satan as lightning fall from heaven, Behold, I give unto you power (Spiritual power) to tread on serpents (Spirits) and scorpions (Spirits) and over all the power of the enemy: and nothing shall by any means hurt you. Notwithstanding, in this rejoice not,

That **the Spirits are subject unto you**; but rather rejoice, because your names are written in heaven. **The Spirits are subject unto you.**

Pray For Yourself

Command those Spirits, To get out of You To Go!

In The Name of Jesus!
Find a person that you trust
To pray with you and assist
You with your prayer.
It can be dangerous to do it alone?
You may want to fast ½ day

Before you do your prayer.

First begin to
Praise and Worship, God,

John 4:2

We must only worship "God."

God is a Spirit, and those who worship "Him" must worship in spirit and truth"

Proclaim your commitment to Jesus Christ by saying:

Father God, I declare that Jesus Is My Lord,
Satan, Demons, Demonic Influence, All Evil Spirits,
Unclean Spirits, Familiar Spirits and Spirits of Bondage, I put you on noticc and I declare this day that Jesus, Is My Lord

The Word of God says in Joel 2:32
Whosoever Shall Call On the Name of the Lord,
Shall be Delivered, Lord Jesus, and I Am Calling upon you today for my Deliverance.

Father God, I ask you to send Holy Angels to assist in binding these Spirits as they are called out, and In the Name of Jesus, I bind all Spirits as your name is called out you are to be bound with chains and fetters of iron covered with a blood covering of the blood of Jesus paralyzing, you and you can not take revenge, retaliate or lash back at me, my family or anything connected with me or us. In the Name of Jesus I command you to leave my Soul, Body Atmosphere and Geographical area bound with all of your dead works actions, thoughts and deeds that I have embraced because of following your lies, temptations and or influences.

In the Name of Jesus, I now renounce and resist all of your endeavors known and unknown and those of your wicked spirits to rob me of the will of God for my life, I terminate your assignment and I cancel your contracts with me or with any of my ancestors made through sins, iniquities or transgressions. I put you on notice that Jesus Christ is my Lord and Savior; I have been bought by the blood of the Lamb. In the Name of Jesus, I apply and sprinkle the blood of Jesus over myself, my family and over every thing that concerns us. I thank you Jesus, you died on the cross for my sins and the third day rose again from the dead for my justification. I repent and I am deeply sorry for all my sins. As I confess them to you right now and I ask you Jesus to deliver me from Spiritual Ignorance by the renewing of my mind soul and body after my spiritual freedom. Holy Spirit, I ask you to expose the areas within my soul, heart, and mind, will, emotions and body that need to be restored to God, through the Casting out of Spirits. Now. **Quietly listen to the Holy Spirit, take a pen and paper list those things that are brought to your mind, write them down below.**

Soul Fragmentation

_____

_____

_____

_____

_____

Forgive me, Lord Jesus. From this day forward, I choose the way the truth and your Life, Light and Love, Thank you, Jesus, for redeeming me with your precious blood and forgiving me for all of my sins. Jesus I know that you love me. God, Father, I know that you love me. Holy Spirit, right now, let your love cover me that the power of God, can flow to me through the love of God for me.

Now;

Ask the Lord Jesus, to examine your heart, to see if there is any hardness in your heart by-way-of-unforgiveness, hatred or revenge. If there is any ask Jesus to help you in that area of unforgiveness, resentment or revenge by taking it away from you through your ability to forgive, name those persons. Forgive them individually.

_____

_____

_____

_____

Ask Jesus to assist you with the power of "His" Blood and "His" Cross, which is to extend his grace and mercy toward you by relieving you and the person or persons that you are holding all of this vileness in your heart towards. Ask Jesus to alleviate them also from the demonic bondage against them by this act.

When Satan, Demons, Fallen Angels, Evil and Unclean, Spirits of Bondage are cast out in the name of Jesus, they are usually expelled on the breath, such as Coughing, Burping, Sneezing, Yawning, Crying, or Sighing, Sometimes even Through Urination, a Bowel movement or a heavy Menstrual cycle. The word for breath and the word for spirit in the Greek are the same word, "Pneuma."

During your Self-Deliverance Prayer I want to ask you to,
Place two or three rolls of paper towels torn apart next to you,
Get a small garbage can or plastic bag, put that right next to your legs.
You need to find a straight back chair uncrossing your legs and arms and get ready.
Now anoint your self with some anointing oil, In the Name of Jesus and prepare to experience some personal freedom.

If you like now you can either play or you can sing a worship song to the Lord Jesus. The blood songs work wonderfully as they help in the deliverance, songs such as;
I Know it was the blood.
The Blood that Jesus shed for me.
Under the blood,
Thank God for the blood, etc.

Now pray this prayer out loud,

Lord God, You said in your word that whosoever shall call upon the
Name of the Lord, Shall be delivered.
I am calling upon you now for my Deliverance.
In the Name of Jesus, Father God, through the blood of Jesus that was Shed for me and by the Power of The Holy Spirit.
I ask you to allow these Satan's, demons, evil spirits, unclean spirits and spirits of bondage to come out of any part of me that has an opening.

First we are going to:

Break All Generational Iniquities, Sins and Transgressions and Command all related Spirits
That came in with them with their seeds and roots to Go!
In Jesus Name

Lord Jesus, According to Exodus 34:7 remove out of me any and all generational spirits aligned with any curses from God for the disobedience, of my fathers, through Iniquities, transgressions and sins. All the seeds and all of the roots of you Spirits, with your thoughts, actions, deeds and works,

Get out of me right now, In The Name of Jesus,
Say Go!
And begin to cough them out, Keep commanding them to Go! Go!
In Jesus name until you feel them released and gone.

Now we are going to
Break, Cast Out and Command all Spirits with the seeds and roots that came in through,
Spiritual Curses from God due to Disobedience and Sins of your Fathers and your self Found in Deut. Chapter 28: 15-68
With you Commanding All of Spirits with their seeds and roots to Go!
In Jesus Name
Lord Jesus in your name and by your blood, I ask you to forgive me and my family line for all of our sins of disobedience and I renounce any claim that Satan, Demons, Unclean, Familiar, and Evil Spirits have put upon me or us, I ask you to forgive me and my blood line all the way back to Adam for all Curses and to release us from their assignments and contracts including all Related Spirits, their thoughts, actions, deeds, and works to leave us Including the Spirits from any Curses of Illegitimate birth and the Spirits Related to the Curse of the bastard, delivering us from any and all spirits of Confusion and Spirits that cause what we put our hands to being cursed, Through spirits of destruction and sudden ruin from the beginning of time to The present.
In the Name of Jesus, I break all Ungodly ties and bonds between my Spirit, Soul and Body, Spirit family connections, Oaths, Covenants, Agreements, Rituals or Spells, made with or without my will against me or my family line.
I command any and all of you Spirits that came in through the Curse of disobedience from God, your Seeds, Roots, works, actions, deeds and thoughts to get out of me, Right Now, Go!
In Jesus Name, All Unclean Spirits, Familiar Spirits, Evil Spirits and Spirits of Bondage,
In the Name of Jesus, Get out of me, Go!
Command those spirits out of you and COUGH those spirits out, Go! Go!

Now we are going to
Break Generational Witchcraft, Curses

We are going to Cast Out and Command all Spirits the seeds and roots that came in through Spiritual Witchcraft Curses

In the Name of Jesus, I break all Ungodly ties and bonds between my Spirit, Soul and Body, Spirit family connections, In Jesus Name I cancel any and all Oaths, Covenants, Agreements, Rituals or Spells, made with or without my will against me through Generational Witchcraft, I command any and all of you Spirits, your Seeds, Roots, works, actions, deeds and thoughts to get out of me, Right Now In Jesus Name, Go!

Lord Jesus In your Name and by your blood, I command out of me, every spirit their, works, thoughts, deeds, actions and effects of , generational witchcraft, from all evil curses of divination, sorcery and wizardry through the use of charms, chains, food, jewelry, art, vexes, hexes, spells, jinxes, psychic powers and prayers, bewitchment, spiritualism, devil worship, new age spirits, soul projection, astral travel levitation, Ouija board spirits, hypnotism, self-hypnosis, black magic, white magic, witchcraft, enemies of God, spirits, Santeria spirits, Reiki, Crystals, DNA Attachments, Voodoo, Hoodoo, Roots and root working curses and spirits necromancy, mind control and sorcery between my body, soul and spirit, along with that of my children.
I command any and all of you spirits to get out of me, Right
Now, Go! All Unclean Spirits, Familiar Spirits, Evil Spirits, Witchcraft spirits,
Get out of me, Right Now, Go! In the Name of Jesus, Command those Spirits to Get out of you, Go!
COUGH those spirits out

Now we are going to
Break Generational Satanic Covenants or Agreements
We are going to Break and Command the Spirits with their seeds and roots that came in through Generational Satanic Covenants or Agreements to Get Out of you. **In the Name of Jesus, I break all Ungodly ties and bonds between my Spirit, Soul and Body, All Spirit family connections, In Jesus Name I cancel any and all Oaths, Covenants, Agreements, Rituals or Spells, made with or without my will against me.** I command any and all of you Spirits, to Get out of me, In the Name of Jesus, your Seeds, Roots, works, actions, deeds and thoughts to get out of me Right Now, Go!
Lord Jesus In Your Name and by your blood, I command out of me any and all spirits, their, works, thoughts, deeds, actions, thoughts and effects, through any agreement or covenant that I have made with Satan and his demons, or that was made on my behalf by any person living or dead, within my family or family line, All the way back to Adam, I now break that covenant of any and all Occult Practices, Rituals or Spells Psychic Spirits and Sources, all related Spirits, Supporting Spirits and hanging on Spirits According to the Power of The Holy Spirit. In The name of Jesus, as these Spirits come out I cut break, sever and loose myself, my family and that of my children's from the beginning of time to the present and I command You Spirits to

get out of me All Unclean Spirits, Familiar Spirits, Spirits of Bondage, Evil Spirits, Right Now, In Jesus Name Go!

Command them to get out of you, tell them to Go!

And COUGH those spirits out

Now we are going to

Cast Out the Spirits that Work with Ungodly Soul-Ties

As we Break the Soul ties and Command all related Spirits with their seeds and roots that came in through the ungodly soul-ties or by way of Agreements with those Soul-ties.

In the Name of Jesus, I break all Ungodly ties and bonds between my Spirit, Soul and Body, Spirit family connections, In Jesus Name I cancel any and all Oaths, Covenants, Agreements, Rituals or Spells, made with or without my will against me. I command any and all of you Spirits, your Seeds, Roots, works, actions, deeds and thoughts connected to all ungodly soul-ties to get out of me Right, Now In Jesus Name Go!

I now command out of me, In The Name of Jesus and by the blood of Jesus any spirit which the devil sent to me when I was in his kingdom through Ungodly soul ties through past sexual partners, of my self and my husband or wife along with all of their, thoughts, works, deeds, actions, and effects. Especially the Spirits of Abuse evil predator spirits, transference of spirits, bad evil, domination spirits, spirits of rebellion, pride, covetousness, lust, perversion, seduction and all sexual spirits

I command you to get out of me All Unclean Spirits, Familiar Spirits, spirits of Bondage and Evil Spirits, Right Now, In Jesus Name, Go!

Command those Spirits to Go!

COUGH those spirits out

Now we are going to

Cast Out Spirits of Free Masonry

Break and Command all Spirits with their seeds and roots that came in through Masons Lodges, Degrees of Masonry, York Rites, Shriners, Council of Princes of Jerusalem, Chapter of the Rose Croix, Council of Kaddosh or Agreements **In the Name of Jesus, I break all Ungodly ties and bonds between my Spirit, Soul and Body, Spirit family connections, In Jesus Name I cancel any and all Oaths, Covenants, Agreements, Rituals or Spells, made with or without my will against me or my family line.**

I command any and all of you Spirits, your Seeds, Roots, works, actions, deeds and thoughts to get out of me.

Lord Jesus in your name and by your blood, I command out of me every spirit their works, thoughts, deeds, actions and effects; of Self-Righteousness, Criticism, judgmentalism Contention, Fighting, Vanity, Arrogance, Manipulation, Bragging, Mockery, and all like spirits.

All Unclean Spirits, Familiar Spirits, Spirits of Bondage and Evil Spirits, Get out of me Now! In the Name of Jesus,

Command those Spirits to Go!
COUGH those spirits out Go!

Now we are going to Cast Out Spirits of Slavery
Break and Command all Spirits with their seeds and roots that came in through Slavery or in Agreements with any Slavery from the beginning of time; **In the Name of Jesus, I break all Ungodly ties and bonds between my Spirit, Soul and Body, Spirit family connections to Slavery, In Jesus Name I cancel any and all Oaths, Covenants, Agreements, Rituals or Spells, made with or without my will against me through any form of Slavery.** I command any and all of you Spirits, your Seeds, Roots, works, actions, deeds and thoughts to get out of me, Lord Jesus in your name and by your blood, I command out of me and away from me every spirit of slavery, fear of hunger, vagabond, rape, sexual promiscuity, self comfort, stealing, gambling, obsession to own land, addiction, alcoholism, survivorship, denial of truth, inferiority, self-loathing, false pride, poverty, lying, deceit, color struck with its, works, deeds, thoughts, and effects, that the enemy has sent to me. I command out of me all spirits of flattery, exaggeration, insinuation, vain imagination, deception, self-deception, false witness and any such like spirits that can enslave spirit, soul or body.
In The Name of Jesus,
I command you spirits to get out of me,
Right Now, Go!
In the Name of Jesus, command All Unclean Spirits, Familiar Spirits, Spirits of Bondage, Evil Spirits, Go!
COUGH those spirits out

Now we are going to
Cast Out Spirits of False Religions and Cults,
In Jesus Name I Command all of you Spirits of false religions and cults with your seeds and roots to get out of me along with any transferring of spirits that may have come in through False Religions, Cults or Agreements **In the Name of Jesus, I break all Ungodly ties and bonds between my Spirit, Soul and Body, Spirit family connections, In Jesus Name I cancel any and all Oaths, Covenants, Agreements, Rituals or Spells, made with or without my will against me.** I command any and all of you Spirits, your Seeds, Roots, works, actions, deeds and thoughts to get out of me,
Right Now, Go!
Lord Jesus in your name and by your blood, I command out of me the perverse spirits of false religions and cults with all of its, effects, thoughts, actions, works and deeds, spirits that pervert the Gospel of Jesus Christ, spirits of false teaching, spirits that cause one failure after another, heresy spirits, blasphemy spirits, spirits of spiritual poverty, spirits that rob me of the blessings of Abraham- and all the material and financial things that God wants me to have through the promises in "His word".

I command you to get out of me All Unclean Spirits, Familiar Spirits, Bondage Spirits, Evil Spirits, Right Now, Go!
In the Name of Jesus,
Command those Spirits to Go!
COUGH those spirits out

Lord Jesus, I command out of me All Spirits the seeds and roots of, Hatred, Rebellion, Anger, Stubbornness, Fighting, Necromancy, Cursing, Religious Spirits, Murder, Heresies, Argumentative Spirits, False Prophecy Spirits and Lying Spirits, Along with every kindred and Supporting Spirit, their works, acts, deeds, thoughts, actions and effects. All spirits of envy, murder, anger, temper, temper tantrums, rage, spite, selfishness, revenge, retaliation, and all like spirits.
In the Name of Jesus I command all of you Spirits to get out of me Now, All Unclean Spirits, Familiar Spirits, Bondage Spirits, Evil Spirits, Right Now, Go!
Command those Spirits to Go!
COUGH those spirits out

Lord Jesus, I command out of me all, Religious Spirits, Murder, Heresies, Spirits that cause a bad Attitude, Girlfriend Spirits, Junk Food Spirits, Boyfriend Spirits, Anorexia, False Marriage, Gluttony Spirits, all of these Spirits along with your seeds and roots In the name of Jesus
Go! I command all of your Works, effects, thoughts, deeds and actions of heaviness, spirit of mourning, sadness, sorrow, grief, crying, loneliness, depression, self-pity, despair, hopelessness, gloominess, discouragement, escapism, suicide and the spirit of death. Get out of me Now, All Unclean Spirits, Familiar Spirits, Bondage Spirits, Evil Spirits, Right Now, Go!
Command those Spirits to Go!
COUGH those spirits out

Lord Jesus, I command out of me all of these Spirits along with their seeds and roots, In Jesus Name
All Spirits of **Infirmity (Luke 13:11)**
Arthritis, Asthma, Bloody flux, Colds, Feeble, Fever, Frailty, Fungus, Hay fever, Hunchback, Impotent, Malady, Sinus, Viral infections, Weak, Divorce, Medication, Polygamy, Depression, Sexual Abuse, Withdrawal, Pedophile, Self-Pity All of your works, deeds, actions, effects and thoughts, especially the spirits of

(Name your particular infirmity)

I command _____ **you to get out of me** All Unclean Spirits, Familiar Spirits, Bondage Spirits, Evil Spirits, **Right Now, Go!**

In Jesus Name Command those Spirits to Go!
COUGH those spirits out

In The Name of Jesus, I command out of me all distressing Spirits, your seeds and roots to Go!
In Jesus Name
Oral Sex, Despair, Adultery, Paranoia
Molestation, Discouragement, Homosexuality, Self-Will,
Lesbianism, Excessive Talkativeness, Jezebel, Unteachable Spirits, **All of your works, actions, deeds, thoughts and effects that cause agony, torment, extreme pain and pressure both mental and physical. I command you to get out of me** All Unclean Spirits, Familiar Spirits, Bondage Spirits, Evil Spirits, **In Jesus Name, Right Now, Go!**
Command those Spirits to Go!
COUGH those spirits out.

Lord Jesus, I command all spirits of Alcoholism, Double Minded, Nicotine, Ego, Anti-Christ, Drugs, Witchcraft, Fear of Rejection, Root of bitterness, Fear of People, Psychics, Anti-Christ, Horoscope, New Age, Clairvoyance, Corrupt Communication **Bondage (Romans 8:15)**
All addictions, False Ambitions, Anguish, Avarice, Bitterness, Blindness, Bound and blocked emotions, Broken heart, Bruised emotions, Captivity, Compulsory Sin, Lust, and Oppression, your works, effects, actions, deeds thoughts, All Of You Spirits your seeds and roots, In the Name of Jesus, Go!
Get out of me now! Go!
In Jesus Name! Go!

In the Name of Jesus, I command all Spirits of bondage to be broken destroyed and lifted off me and my family. I bind, break and loose myself from the power of all spirits of bondage, spirits that do not let me obey the truth, spirits that prevent me from taking a stand for Jesus. Or bondage to addiction to tobacco, to drugs-legal and ill legal drugs, alcohol, sweets, caffeine, gluttony, sexual addictions, internet addictions **(Now name your own form of bondage)**

_____

_____

I command you to get out of me All Unclean Spirits, Familiar Spirits, Bondage Spirits, Evil Spirits, In the Name of Jesus, Right Now, Go!
Command those Spirit to Go!
COUGH those spirits out.

Lord Jesus, I command out of me, all spirits of **Fear** the seeds and roots of all fear to Get out of me! Go!

In Jesus Name

(II Timothy 1:7)

Agitation, Anxiety, Apprehension, Carefulness, Death, Dread, Faithless, Fear of man, Fear of poverty, Fright, Heart attacks, Horror, Inadequacy, Inferiority, Nightmares, Phobia, Shyness, Tension, Timidity, Torment, Trembling, and Worry terror, fright, trembling, dread, nightmares, and all like spirits. The works, actions, deeds, thoughts and effects, especially the fear of,

(Name your area of fear, what ever it is).

_____

I command all spirits of fear to get out of me All Unclean Spirits, Familiar Spirits, Bondage Spirits, Evil Spirits, In the Name of Jesus, Right Now, Go!

Command those Spirits to Go!

COUGH those spirits out.

Lord Jesus, I command out of me, all Spirits their works, actions, deeds, thoughts, effects the seeds and roots. All Spirits of **Whoredoms (Hosea 4:12)** Harlotry **(Ezekiel 16:28)**, Idolatry **(Matthew 6:21)**, Love of food **(Romans 16:18)**, Love of money **(I Timothy 6:3-10)**, Love of body, Love of the world in any way, shape, or form! **(II Timothy 4:10)**.

Lust, fantasy lust, perversion, fornication, adultery, masturbation, sodomy, incest, rape, homosexuality, lesbianism, anal sex, sex with animals, sex with spirits, succubus and incubus, pan, harpies, Lust of the eyes, pornography, masturbation, internet sex, prostitution, and any and all like spirits,

I command all of you Spirits to get out of me All Unclean Spirits, Familiar Spirits, Bondage Spirits, Evil Spirits, in Jesus Name, Get out of me Right Now, Go!

Command those Spirits to Go!

COUGH those spirits out.

Lord Jesus, I command out of me the spirits, their works, actions, thought, deeds, effects their seeds and roots of Abortion, the spirit that sheds innocent blood, the spirit of Baal, Molech, of child sacrifice, In Jesus Name. I command the works, actions, deeds, thoughts and effects out of me from these Spirits, the spirit that devises wicked plans, the Spirit of Jezebel, that divides, controls and manipulates, the spirit that causes my feet to run to evil, that spreads evil tidings, the spirit that causes me to spread any kind of discord among the brethren.

In the Name of Jesus, I command you to Get out of me All Unclean Spirits, Familiar Spirits, Bondage Spirits, Evil Spirits, Right Now, Go!

COUGH those spirits out.

In the Name of Jesus and by The Power of The Holy Spirit, I command out of me, All Spirits with their seeds and roots
Their works, thoughts, deeds, actions and effects under the authority of Abaddon, or Apollyon, The Destroyer, The Terminator the Angel of the bottomless pit, the Tormentor, In Jesus Name I command these spirits to be powerless bound with any regard to me and my family and everything that concerns us, I Thank you Jesus that these spirits and their works, actions, deeds, thoughts and effects are bound and their assignments, cancelled, terminated against me or my family
I command all you Spirits and supporting Spirits to Get out of me All Unclean Spirits, Familiar Spirits, Bondage Spirits, Evil Spirits, Get out of me Right Now, In Jesus Name, Go!
Command those Spirits to Go!
COUGH those spirits out

In The Name of Jesus, I command out of me all spirits their works, thoughts, deeds, actions, effects the seeds and roots
Of Deception, all doctrines of demons, all Spirits of **CURSING** - blasphemy, course jesting, gossip, criticism, backbiting, mockery, belittling, railing, (La' Shan hara, speaking forth Satan's kingdom in any way, shape, or form)--added by Issachar Prophet ritualism, formalism, doctrinal error, legalism, super religiosity, seducing spirits, and all Spirits of mind control, mind binding spirits, spirits of Another Jesus, Angels of Light, Spirits of The Dead and of The New Age Movement.
In the Name of Jesus, I command you to, Get out of me All Unclean Spirits, Familiar Spirits, Bondage Spirits, Evil Spirits, Right Now, Go!
Command those Spirits to Go!
COUGH those spirits out

In the name of Jesus, I command out of me the spirits of **Deaf and Dumb (Mark 9:25)** deep sleep, forgetfulness, Indifference, procrastination, laziness, confusion, spirits That do not let me understand the word of God, spirits that Cause me to get drowsy when I hear the Word of God.
Spirits of doubt, unbelief, skepticism, Blindness, Bruising, Burn, Convulsions, Diseases, Drown, Dumbness, Epilepsy, Foaming, Gnashing, Hydrophobia, Insanity, Lunatic, Madness, Prostration, Schizophrenia, Seizures, and Suicidal **Heaviness (Isaiah 61:3)** Bruised, Despair, Discouragement, Gloominess, Gluttony, Grief, Hopelessness, Loneliness, Mourning, Rejection, Self pity, Sorrow or sadness, and Troubled Spirits, Anger, Competition, Coveting, Cruelty, Emulation, Hate, Murder, Rage, Revenge, Selfishness, Spite, Suspicions, Variance, and Wrath.
all of these Spirits with their works, actions, deeds, thoughts and effects of stupor, gross

stupidity, slumbering spirits, the spirits that causes me to be slow of speech, slow to understand or learn, and all like spirits.

In the name of Jesus, I command you to Get out of me All Unclean Spirits, Familiar Spirits, Bondage Spirits, Evil Spirits, Right Now Get out of me, Go!

Command those Spirits to Go!

COUGH those spirits out.

In the Name of Jesus, I command out of me the works, deeds, actions, thoughts and deeds of all Witchcraft **Divination and Familiar Spirits (I Samuel 28:7-8)** Astrology, Clairvoyance, Conjurer, Witch or Wizard, Enchanter, Hypnotist, Medium, Mimicry, Mutterer, Necromancer, Pantomiming, Peeping Tom, Soothsayer, Stargazer, Teraphim, and Ventriloquist. All Nature Spirits, fairies, elves and water spirits any and all Airways Spirits sent by any Witch, Warlock, Coven, Wizard, Sorcerer or Spiritualist.

I command you to Get out of me All Unclean Spirits, Familiar Spirits, Bondage Spirits, Evil Spirits, In the Name of Jesus, Get Out of me, Right Now, Go!

Command those Spirits to Go!

COUGH those spirits out.

In the name of Jesus, I command out of me the spirits, their works, actions, deeds, thoughts and effects of The Anti-Christ, False Trinity, False Prophecy and all Falsehoods, Including false teaching, all related stubbornness and Rebellion and all like spirits. **Lying (II Chronicles 18:22)**

Driving Zeal, Ecclesiastical, Exaggeration, Flattery, Frenzied, Hypocrisy, Insinuation, La'shan hara, Old wives' Tales, Pharisaic, Profanity, Religious, Strong delusion, Superstitions, Vain babblings and Vain imagination.

In the Name of Jesus, I command you to Get out of me All Unclean Spirits, Familiar Spirits, Bondage Spirits, Evil Spirits right now, Go!

Command those Spirits to Go!

COUGH those spirits out.

In the name of Jesus, I command out of me, the spirits their works, deeds, actions, thoughts and effects with their seeds and roots of Nehushtan (serpent on a pole) Num 21:8,9, 2 Kings 18:4, John 3:14,15 religiosity, doctrinal error, legalism, ritualism, formalism, pageantry, amulets and all False religion. spiritual superiority Arrogance, Bragging, Contention, Doctorial, Egotistical, Exalted feelings, Gossip, Holier-than-thou, Insolent, Lofty looks, Mockery, Proud, Scornful, Self-assertion, Self-righteousness, Stiff-necked, Vanity and Wrathful. In the Name of Jesus, I command you to Get out of me All Unclean Spirits, Familiar Spirits, Bondage Spirits, Evil Spirits right now, Go!

Command those spirits to Go!

COUGH those spirits out.

The Spirits Are Subject Unto You

Lord Jesus, I command out of me all spirits their works, thoughts, deeds, actions, effects their seeds and roots of Nephillim, Gibborim, Giants mighty men of renown. Science Fiction, UFO's, Aliens, Extra terrestrials, Hybrids, crop Circles, conspiracy, rebellion to authority, alien and UFO Movies, and TV Shows, Abductions, Astral and Soul travel, Ghosts, horror, Movies, remote writing, Lochness, Big foot, Psychic brain waves, Brain suggestions and weird body Movements. All of the doctrines of demons. WIVES and BRIDES OF SATAN, ALL SPIRITS OF ANTI-LIFE, All Unknown Spirits of bondage, domination, manipulation and control.

In the Name of Jesus, I command you to Get out of me All Unclean Spirits, Familiar Spirits, Bondage Spirits, Evil Spirits right now, Go!

Command those Spirits to Go!

COUGH those spirits out.

Now stop begin to Thank and Praise God!

Every time you command evil and unclean spirits to leave, you should always invite the Holy Spirit to take the place of those spirits that you have cast out, re-filling that area   In Jesus Name.

Pray This Prayer

"Father God, In the Name of Jesus,
I ask for the Holy to
Spirit, to fill me with all that you are, I ask this through the grace that you have extended to me, I need to be filled with Your Compassion,
Your Love, your Joy, your Peace, your
Long Suffering, your Kindness, your
Goodness, your Gentleness, your
Faithfulness and your Self-Control.
Thank you,
Father, In Jesus Name, I am being filled right now.
Lord Jesus, restore my soul and restore to me the Joy of the Lord, Give me the Oil of Joy for mourning, the Joy of knowing you, the Joy of working in your kingdom, the Joy of becoming a soul winner, the Joy of being called a tree of righteousness so that you, Jesus may be glorified.
I ask this in your Name Jesus, The Name above all names.
Now I Thank you that I am being filled with the Joy of the Lord.
Holy Spirit fill every empty area OF MY SPIRIT, SOUL AND BODY with your power, light, life and Glory.
Thank You Jesus

Discerning of Spirits Gift

The Spiritual realm exists and is made up of God, and a whole and complete realm of Spiritual existence, with God, being ruler over everything Natural and Spiritual. God has given us a special ability to discern and judge the spiritual things revealed by Him, through our Spirits. By The Gift of Discerning of Spirits, which generally comes as a Gift of The Holy

Spirit. This is a valuable aid from The Holy Spirit allowing us the Spiritual ability to tell whether something is of the flesh (that is human motivation) of The Holy Spirit, or of demonic spiritual influence. It is mentioned in The Word of God in 1 Cor.12:10 "To another the working of miracles, to another prophecy; to another Discerning of Spirits…The Greek word for 'discern" here is "diakrsis" which according to Vine' Expository Dictionary (171) means "a distinguishing, a clear discrimination, discerning, judging…Of Spirits, judging by evidence whether they are evil from Satan or good from God. The Gift of Discerning of Spirits is given by The Holy Spirit as a result of having received the Baptism in The Holy Spirit. There are basically two kinds of "Baptisms" of the Holy Spirit. The Baptism by the Spirit you receive when you are saved; you are baptized into the Body of Christ. "For you were baptized by one Spirit into one Body: This is the Spirit Baptism that makes us "one". As a result, the Holy Spirit indwells us and we have this seal of redemption. Then there is the Baptism in the Holy Spirit, where the Holy Spirit comes upon you and fills you with power. Acts 1; 8 and where the gifts of the Spirit become available to you as give to us in 1 Cor. 12. There are several Gifts; however, I will only elaborate on, the gift of Discerning of Spirits. As this gift often manifest or reveals itself in many Spiritual variations, and is given to the Spirit-filled-believer to help them distinguish spiritual good from spiritual evil and spiritual truth from spiritual falsehood that is operating from within the spiritual realm. This gift comes as an inner-knowing, the Holy Spirit witnesses to your spirit man (inner-man) and in your mind; you get spiritual understanding, and however this is not the only inner-man understanding that you receive. It also comes through **Spiritually Hearing;** allows you the spiritual ability to hear things beyond the range of the normal perception of our physical ears. Such as conversations, hearing the music of the angels, hearing inner profound messages and words from the Holy Spirit. **Spiritually Feelings; possessing the gifting from God of being able to** feel with an inner spiritual, sensing, inspired feelings from the Holy Spirit. **Spiritually Sensing; having the ability from God to** feel, sense and know the Physical, Mental, an Emotional, sensations of another person, having the spiritual ability to feel the attitudes and inner dispositions of the Spirits of those people that are around you both good and bad. **Spiritually Knowing;** Spiritually knowing without having a logical reason for knowing because the knowing is from the Holy Spirit, to our spirit with a clear knowing, including meaning and information. **Spiritually smelling; having the spiritual ability to clearly through the Holy Spirit smell odors and fragrances that that are not within our immediate surrounding.** Such as the smelling of the fragrance of roses when the presence of Jesus is there. This gift many times works along with the ability to taste without putting anything in our mouths. **Not enough is taught about this gift, this spiritual gifting seems to flow through my ministry along with the "seer" Gift with a special anointing for Exorcism and Deliverance Miracles.** Through this gifting, the Holy Spirit will allow you to discern the very desires of the hearts of men and women, so that you can be used as the vessel of God to bless them, In The Name of Jesus. **The Gift of Discerning manifests or reveals it's self in the form of Visions and Dreams also.** An individual may see an image or a picture normally with their eyes closed but sometimes even with their eyes wide open, What is seen is not Physical but Spiritual in nature, seeing, beyond what he physical eyes can see; visionary ability to see into the Spiritual realm or the Heavenly realm. The God given gift with the ability to see straight into the Spiritual realm or the Heavenly realm. The God given gift with the ability to see worldly beings, lights, shapes and colors. God does not let us see like this all the time, but the thing that we have to remember is that the Spiritual or Heavenly realm is always in operation, parallel to the physical realm all the time. There are examples of people reaching out or seeing things within the Spiritual realm understanding the meanings of messages. And having the ability to receive Heavenly messages. Perceive visions, sometimes as if you are right there within the midst of what is going on, or at other times looking at things being enacted out in front of you as if you are watching television, at a play or attending a movie. I am not mixing this gift up with any of the other Gifts of the Spirit, our ministry flows in all of them as well. However, at this time, I am writing about the Spiritual Gifting through the Gift of Discerning of Spirits. **Stephen in Acts, chapter 6 and 7 was given the Spiritual ability enabling him to see into the Heavenly realm.** As the early Church increased in size, so did its needs. One great need that arose was to organize the distribution of food for the poor. The apostles needed to focus on preaching so they choose others to administer the food. This administrative task was not taken lightly the requirements for the men who were to handle the food program was; That they were to have an honest report; be full of the Holy Ghost and Wisdom. One of the men that they chose was a man name Stephen and The Word of God says that He was a man full of faith and power. And that Stephen did great wonders and miracles among the people. The word of God says that the people were not able to resist the Wisdom and Spirit by which he spoke. A group of Jewish slaves who had been freed by Rome and had formed their own synagogue lied about Stephen. Thus causing Stephen to be arrested and brought before the Sadducees. When Stephen was brought before the Sanhedrin council the accusation against him was the same accusation that the religious leaders had used against Jesus. The group falsely accused Stephen of wanting to change Moses customs, because they knew that the Sadducees, who controlled the council, believe only in Moses laws. Stephen launched into a long speech about Israel's relationship with God. Stephen didn't really defend himself; instead he took offensive, seizing the opportunity to summarize his teachings about Jesus. Those people became so angry that they charged Stephen. But in Chapter 7, verse 55 it says, but he (Stephen) being full of the Holy Ghost, looked up steadfastly into heaven, and saw, the glory of God, and Jesus standing on the right hand of God. And said, Behold, I see the heavens opened, and the Son of man standing on the right hand of God. Stephen had the heavenly or spiritual realm opened for him to see into by God. And the Word of God said that Stephen was full of faith, and He Saw. Jesus healed ten, men with Leprosy Read Luke Chapter 17 verses 11 through 19. This story has a spiritual meaning that was faith motivated and spiritually orchestrated by God. Whereby people are receiving from the Heavenly or Spiritual realm from God that which was needed here in the physical realm. People who had leprosy were required to try to stay away from other people and to announce their presence if they had to come near. Sometimes leprosy went into remission. If a leper thought his leprosy had gone away, he was supposed to present himself to a priest who could declare him clean. Jesus sent the ten lepers to go and show themselves to the high priest before they wee healed an act of faith. Can you imagine what would have happened if the ten lepers had turned up in the high priests office without being healed. In going they responded in faith to Jesus' instructions and Jesus healed them on their way. Jesus knew that the leper's healing was already a done and concluded miracle. As they went by faith to the high priest they received an outward manifestation of their inward healing and we need to understand that the provision had already been made for them by God the Father in the Spiritual or Heavenly realm. They received in their physical bodies within the natural realm here on earth that which was already provided for them from the Spiritual realm into their physical bodies. Jesus had already healed all ten lepers from the moment that he spoke to them and they turned from him in obedience and faith toward the high priests they were already healed. **The Prophet Elisha had the ability to hear from and see into the Spiritual or Heavenly realm. 2 Kings Chapter 6 verses 8 through 17 clearly illustrates to us this Spiritual ability from God and its effect bringing about provision and protection for God's people. Elisha had the gift and ability from God to speak into the Spiritual or Heavenly realm through prayer and receive the desired results of the prayer from out of the Heavenly or Spiritual realm of God into the natural realm of the earth.** The king of Aram was at war with Israel; Elisha the man of God sent word of the King of Israel informing him of Aram's battle plans over and over again, the word of God says. The King of Aram became enraged and was told that Elisha the Prophet was telling the King of Israel the very words that he was speaking in his bedroom. So the king set out to find the Prophet and capture him. He sent horses and chariots and a strong force out to capture him. When Elisha got up early in the morning and went out of his house. King Aram's army with horses and chariots had surrounded the city and Elisha's servant saw this and became afraid. Verse 16 and 17 says, and he (Elisha) answered, "Fear not; for they that be with us are more than they that be with them (King Aram's army). And Elisha prayed, and said, Lord I pray thee open his eyes, that he may see. And the Lord opened the eyes of the young man; and he saw and, behold, the mountain was full of horses and chariots of fire round about Elisha. Elisha's servant's eyes of faith opened in answer to Elisha's prayer. He then saw God's provision which had already been made for God's people in the Spiritual or Heavenly realm revealed and made visible in the natural realm. Verse 18 says, "And when they came down to him, Elisha prayed unto the Lord, and said smite this people, I pray thee with blindness. And He (God) smote them with blindness according to the Word of Elisha. Verse 20 and it came to pass, when they were come into Samaria, that Elisha said, **"Lord open the eyes of these men that they may see. And the Lord opened their eyes, and they saw; and** behold they were in the midst of Samaria. **Speaking into the Spiritual or Heavenly realm. The Apostle Paul experienced a spiritual conversion to the Lord Jesus Christ. It begins in the 9th Chapter of Acts. As Saul who later became Saul traveled to Damascus, in his quest of persecuting Christians he was confronted (Spiritually) by "The risen Jesus Christ" and brought face to face with the truth of the Gospel. Paul refers to this (Spiritual0 experience as the start of his new life in Christ. At the center of this wonderful experience is "Jesus,"** Paul did not see a vision, he saw the Risen Jesus Christ himself. Paul acknowledged Jesus as Lord, confessed his own sin, surrendered his life to Jesus Christ and resolved to obey him. There is mention of a special filling of the Holy Spirit for Saul, In Acts 9:16-18 it says, God speaking to Ananias his obedient servant, instructing him to go and lay his hands upon Paul. "For I will shew him how great things he must suffer for my name's sake." And Ananias went his way, and entered into the house; and putting his hands on him said," Brother Saul, the Lord, even Jesus, that appeared unto thee in the way as thou camest, hath sent me, that thou mightest receive thy sight, and be filled with the Holy Ghost. And immediately there fell from his eyes as it had been scales and he received sight forthwith, and arose and was baptized." Paul's life being changed and his subsequent accomplishments bear strong witness to the Holy Spirit's continued presence and power in his life. **There is therefore now no condemnation to them which are in Christ Jesus, who walk not after the flesh, but after the Spirit. For the law of the Spirit of life in Christ Jesus hath made me free from the law of sin and death. For what the law could not do, in that it was weak through the flesh, God sending his own Son in the likeness of sinful flesh, and for sin, condemned sin in the flesh: that the righteousness of the law might be fulfilled in us, who walk not after the flesh, but after the Spirit. For they that are after the flesh do mind the things of the flesh; but they that are after the Spirit the things of the Spirit. For to be carnally minded is death; but to be spiritually minded is life and peace. Because the carnal mind is enmity against God: for it is not subject to the law of God, neither indeed can be. So then they that are in the flesh cannot please God. But ye are not in the flesh, but in the Spirit, if so be that the Spirit of God dwell in you. Now if any man have not the Spirit of Christ, he is none of his. And if Christ be in you, the body is dead because of sin; but the Spirit is life because of righteousness. But if the Spirit of him that raised up Jesus from the dead dwell in you, he that raised up Christ from the dead shall also quicken your mortal bodies by "HIS" Spirit that dwelleth in you. Romans 8:1-11. Blessed be the God and Father of Our Lord Jesus Christ, who hath Blessed us with all Spiritual Blessings in Heavenly places in**

Christ. (Ephesians 1:3)

Pray the following Pray to receive the Third Person of the Trinity

The Holy Spirit who will endue you with Power from God to be

An effective Witness for Jesus

Power to Overcome the Wiles and Spirits of the Devil.

Suggested Prayer to Receive the Baptism in

The Holy Spirit

Lord Jesus, I love you and I desire more of you, because of my love for you, I come to you as the Baptizer in The Holy Spirit. In obedience to your Word, I ask you to empower me to become a witness, for your great commission. I believe that you provide us with all that you require of us, if we will trust and obey you as an act of our will. Therefore I as an act of my will, and in obedience to your word.

I present myself as living sacrifice, wholly and acceptable unto you, which is my reasonable service. I ask you Lord Jesus because of my love for you. To Baptize me with the Holy Ghost and with fire. Lord Jesus, give me the evidence of speaking in other tongues, as The Holy Spirit gives me the utterance. Lord Jesus, I now receive this Gift by my faith that is by a complete and total trust in you as my Lord and Savior. Amen.

Now lift up your hands to God, and Let the Holy Spirit well up within your innermost being and rise up and begin to flow out of your mouth. In The Name of Jesus. **If you have already been filled with**

The Holy Spirit. Ask God, In the name of Jesus,

To give you the Gift

Discerning of Spirits.

Now believe that you have received and

Begin to Thank Jesus

Spiritual Curses From God

That Can Cause You To Inherit and be Plagued With Evil and Demonic Spirits

Deuteronomy 11:26-28 See, I am setting before you today a blessing and a curse: the blessing if you listen to the commandments of the Lord your God, which I am commanding you today: and the curse, if you do not listen to the commandments of the Lord your God, but turn aside from the way which I am commanding you today, by following other gods which you have not known. Spiritual Curses that come from God take effect when you or your ancestors have committed certain acts which are contrary to the Word of God. An act of sin which then brings **Curses (Judgment from God)** on you and your descendants. These curses are referred to as being on someone for breaking particular aspects of God's laws. Deuteronomy 28:15-68 describes them as the following and in various operations. **Curses for Disobedience;** Food provisions, fruit of the womb and fruit of the ground, travel, disasters, panic, frustrations, disease and wasting disease, fevers, inflammation, weather cursed, and crop disease. Defeat, tumors, festering sores, itch, madness, blindness. Confusion, marriage plans destroyed. Plans for a new home unfulfilled. Children put into bondage, cruel oppression all your days. Madness and boils, becoming an object of scorn and ridicule. Your efforts being fruitless, others will succeed where you fail. The Curses will pursue and bring destruction, dire poverty. You will serve your enemies, national humiliation and defeat, fearful plagues, prolonged disasters, severe and lingering illnesses, no repose, no resting place, anxiety of mind, weary and longing heart, despairing heart, filled with dread day and night, (curses can cause a person to never be sure of there life.) In these cases the curse is a form of judgment for disobedience and rebellion. Whenever we sin we move outside of God's covering and we place ourselves, therefore under the covering of Satan and at this point Satan and his host of Demonic, Spirits will then try to perpetuate the curse for al remaining generations of descendants of our family line. The Devil and his hosts can then enter a child in the womb at the very time of conception. The child then enters life with these characteristics that are demonic. The world's explanation is to say that the; Child inherited this characteristic from his or her ancestors. **In actuality what was inherited was an Evil Demonic Spirit, a Familiar Spirit or Spirits that were passed down from one generation to the next generation, through the blood line the seed of that particular family. We all live with the results of our sins. Blessings are the results of obeying God. Curses on the other hand are the results of obeying the devil and disobeying God. We live in a cursed world, there are people who are cursed all around us and many of these people curse others.** Curses and the Evil spirits that Satan sends to implement them, come into a person through the open door of sin. Anytime a person does not obey the Word of God, there is a curse connected to that act of rebellion. As Deuteronomy 27:26 says 'Cursed is the one who does not confirm all the words of this law. And all the people shall say, AMEN **Cures go all the way back to Adam and Eve and the Garden of Eden.** Genesis 3:1-7 "Now the serpent was more subtle than any beast of the field which the Lord God had made. In the Garden of Eden the serpent talked to the woman Eve and the serpent was successful in getting the woman to sin by listening to him and responding to his temptation which he presented to her as Satan the serpent or the deceiver. Genesis 3: 8-22 "Because of their sin of disobedience in failing to obey God, Adam and Eve were responsible for bringing, sin, negativity, fear, lying, pride, fear and many other bad things upon the whole human race including **Curses from God** Genesis 3:14 "And the Lord God said unto the serpent, because thou has done this, **Thou art cursed** above all cattle, and above every beast of the field; upon thy belly shalt thou go, and dust shalt thou eat all the days of thy life." And unto Adam he said, because thou has hearkened unto the voice of thy wife, and hast eaten of the tree, of which I commanded thee, saying, thou shalt not eat of it; **Cursed is the ground for thy sake;** in sorrow shalt thou eat of it all the days of thy life." **However, I want you to take note of the manner of God's great love for his creation Man and Woman. In spite of man's sin, God did not Curse man.** God is Love and God abides in love and because love is his nature, our relationship with God is founded on Love and Trust. Secondly for Love and Trust to exist at all, there must be the free choice of a free will. And the Lord God said, Behold the man is become as one of us, to know good and evil: One important aspect of man's uniqueness amongst God's creatures is the area of choice that has been entrusted to him. True animals make certain choices, but their choices are locked into patterns of behavior that are essentially instinctive. They are part of the adaptive response of the animal to its environment. Man is different, God the uncreated creator, making man in "His" own image and after "His" own likeness, made man a created creator. That is man can make choices that are creative. Man can choose his own goals. Man can decide what he will become. The behavior of an animal can be changed or modified only by conditioning. An animal can learn. A horse can be broken to the saddle and a puppy can be house-trained. Only man, however, can make moral choices, that decisions of his or her will that are based, not on instinct or conditioning, but on values or standards or right or wrong. Therefore only man can sin. Only man has the freedom of choice that makes moral behavior or misbehavior possible. Here then is the full disclosure of Satan' intention in the Garden of Eden when he tempted man to snatch his "freedom." He was a murderer from the beginning." John 8:44 /this then is one of God's truths, freedom must always be expressed within the limits laid down by law. We call this obedience. Disobedience, or flouting the law, means that the law becomes our enemy and we are no longer free. This is how moral and spiritual laws work within the universe. The Word of God says that the law of the Lord is perfect, it is not something that God made up; it is the way God is. The law of God is the law of unselfish love. It is the expression of the wonderful character of God and it is the way that God chooses to live. **I am going to share a couple of examples of the many people that I personally have ministered to helping them to receive freedom from the Spiritual repercussions of Generational Curses.** In Los Angeles, California, while in a revival service a woman heart about the service and called me at the Church. She explained to me that she was a practicing witch; she said that she had been practicing witchcraft as long as she could remember she said that she dressed as a witch every Halloween as a child. She said that she could always see and know things and that her family encouraged her so she studied to become the most post powerful witch that she could become. This woman told me that she wanted Jesus in her heart and she knew that. What she said that she didn't know was why after she had been to so many people to pray for her that she was so unsuccessful in maintaining a relationship with Jesus. She also told me that if I tried to help her I had better be real and have some power, because everyone that had tried to help her before had failed and something bad had happened to all of them. I told her that I could not help her, but that I knew someone that had all power in heaven and in earth and all power over everything under the earth to deliver her and that was Jesus. If she would be willing to submit to Jesus' authority and power putting her trust in Jesus, who had come into her heart and had become her personal lord and savior that day. That all of her trust had to be in Jesus alone and that if she could do that, then Jesus could use me to help her. That girl came to my meeting that night and she brought another witch with her. She later told me that she had fear of coming and that voices were telling her not to come, she had brought this other witch for reinforcement. Satan's plan was for them to bind me up and bring confusion and destruction into the meeting, they were then going to deny the power of God and transfer their witchcraft spirits upon the Christians that were attending the meeting. The witches sat on the front row. Witches love to sit on the front rows of powerful Church meetings where a move of God is taking place because they are power crazy Well that night I dealt with the witchcraft spirits and about a legion others both withes received exorcism, healing, deliverance and inner-healing, freeing them enough so that they could come back the next 7 days for the same thing each night. During those ministry sessions I found out that she was a fifth generation witch, in effect she had been born into witchcraft (black and white magic) along with her two sisters. This was a generational curse that was not going to go away without a fight. The following week the ministry anointing was so great on this family that Satan tried to murder another sister in that family who was a police officer she tried to commit suicide and did not know why. The Lord Jesus had us get there in time we ministered a Salvation message to her and she and her whole family were marvelously Saved and Delivered. The baby sister in this family was a beautiful fashion model, but she could not keep a husband she was on her fifth husband. She got saved exorcised, delivered and received inner-healing the generational curse was broken she is still married today and it has been 11 years now. **Another example of a Generational Curse being broken and the person delivered from those demons and their demonic influence that I encountered and was very unusual.** A woman came for prayer this woman told me that she was a prophetess and a very recognized minister in her church in New Mexico. She said that she knew something was not right in her ministry life but here prophesies were always one hundred percent accurate. She said that she had been praying and praying with no results, so she thought that she would seek deliverance. I kept getting witchcraft from the Holy Spirit and the lady kept telling me that she had never had anything to do with witchcraft. Ten I asked her about her family and this is the story that came out during months of exorcisms, deliverances, deliverances and inner-healing taking place. She told me that **her** Father had met her Mother and had fallen in love with her Mother and married her, after they had been married for six years and she had not conceived they desperately **wanted a baby. So her Mother told her Father's mother about the situation** What is interesting here is what follows, Her Grandmother on her Father's side told her Mother that she too had been unable to conceive for ten years before she became pregnant with her son, which was now her husband that she was unable to get pregnant from. The Grandmother went on to tell the prophetess's mother that she had gone to an Indian lady to get a potion to help her conceive her husband and it worked. She also told her that she could take her to the reservation because the lady was still living and that she would help her also. Within thirteen month she had a bouncing baby boy which was the Father of lady that I was ministering to. What her Grandmother failed to tell her daughter-in-law was that her son had a lot of severe mental problems. Her Mother got pregnant and gave birth to the lady that I was praying for her Father started sexually molesting her at age 5 selling her as a child prostitute from 10-13 while still molesting her himself. This lady had engaged in every kind of deviate sexual perversion that you could think of and she did not have the power to stop herself from these horrible acts on here own. She was a Grand Worthy Matron in an Eastern Star Lodge. No she did not practice ritualistic witchcraft, but she was a witch using manipulation and powerful mind control, she was a pathological liar, and home wrecker, rumor monger, nymphomaniac, and she prayed psychic prayers (witchcraft) against other Christians and had sex with animals. The Jezebel Spirit had a stronghold within this lady all the while she was the most reliable and steadfast worker in her Church she always seemed to have an abundance of energy in her leadership capacity in every religious organization that she belonged to and there were several. During her exorcisms and deliverances we learned that she had been born a witch through no fault of her own, the Indian Witch had offered the soul in exchange for the ability to conceive a baby. A generational curse was in the process of resisting the salvation of Jesus, later on her Mother was set-free from the witchcraft curse, but her Father resisted and died before salvation, her children were later delivered from generation lust, perversion and whoredom curses. (Her son was a convicted rapist) (Her daughter a prostitute.) **Although I have many stories of Exorcisms and Deliverances from generational curses, I am going to share one other example with you.** I met a youth minister in one of my meetings, a young man that came up to me in the prayer line and asked for prayer for deliverance, but he said that he would be too embarrassed to receive it in the prayer line in front of all the people in the Church that he ministers to. So I agreed to pray for him privately. He made an appointment with me for personal ministry. He came and was on time. I later found out that His dad was the Pastor of a very large Church in that town. I asked him what the problem was and he told me that a woman comes and has sex with him at night and now it was so bad that he was not doing well in his job because he wasn't getting sleep at night but was having sex. I asked him if he was masturbating, he said that he used to but that he didn't have to do that any more because of the lay, he said that she was very beautiful and sexy, he said that he went to talk with his father about it but he said that he already knew because she had been having sex with him too and before that he had gone to his father (the youth ministers grandfather) who also had sex with this woman. He said that he didn't understand. I did this was a Succubus Spirit a familiar spirit with a generational stronghold on this family. This spirit was allowed to operate because the family did nothing about it. The Father did not believe tat an Evil spirit could torment a Christian, besides that he liked the pleasure of it and thought it was some sort of blessing. It took three weeks to get that young man exorcised, delivered and healed from that demonic spiritual stronghold. The youth minister was finally able to convince his Father of the validity of Exorcism, Deliverance, Inner-healing ministry and He got pray and was set free also. **Many of God's people today are suffering because of curses directed against them or in their blood line. Many people don't know how these Curses have invaded their lives, or how to fight the power of these curses.** I personally believe that Deuteronomy Chapter 27 and 28 covers just about all of the curses from God for the sin of disobedience. Since a curse is the opposite of a blessing, one cursed by God can expect blessings to be withdrawn, and a diminishing of the enjoyment God yearns to provide for his children. God threatens his curses in the context of sin and disobedience. Since we all have sinned against God, we all lie under the curse of God. Jesus Christ, by his death on the cross, has won release from the curse of God, from the curse of the law, which no one could keep perfectly. Instead of a curse, believers are supposed to experience rich blessings in Jesus, freedom fullness, and the privilege of being fruitful for the Lord Jesus Christ. Everyone who stubbornly refuses to believe the Good News of Jesus, however, continues to lie under the curse of God. Anytime a person does not obey the Word of God, there is a curse connected to that act of rebellion. As Deuteronomy 27:26 says "Cursed is the one who does not confirm all the words of this law. And all the people shall say, Amen" Then there are some sins that some people do not consider to be sin. For example anger, some would say that anger is an emotion. Yes it is but if a person disobeys the Word of God concerning anger than the door is opened to sin and the person is open to a curse. Ephesians 4:2627 says "Be angry, and do not sin. Do not let the sun go down on your wrath nor give place to the devil." Often, because of resentment and unforgiveness in our hearts, many of us are cursed with various infirmities. Another thing that opens the door to curses is the wearing of amulets or good-luck charms on your body, or having them in your home. Deuteronomy 7:25-6 says "you shall burn the carved images of their Gods with fire; you shall not covet the silver or gold that is on them, nor take it for yourselves, lest you be snared by it; for it is an abomination to the Lord your God. Nor shall you bring an abomination into your house, lest you be doomed to destruction like it; but you shall utterly detest it and abhor it, for it is and accursed thing." Deuteronomy 18: 10-13, clearly tells us that any involvement in any form of occultism is an abomination to the Lord Our God. "There shall not be found among you anyone who makes his son or his daughter pass through the fire, or one who practices witchcraft, or a sooth sayer, or one who interprets omens, or a sorcerer, or one who conjures spells, or a medium, or a spiritist, or one who calls up the dead. For all who do these things are an abomination to the Lord and because of these abominations the Lord your God drives them out from before you. You shall be blameless before the Lord your God." **We can also inherit curses in our blood lines from our Ancestors; we were in our Father's loins, in our Grandfather's loins, in our Great Grandfathers loins, etc. A curse can come in as far back generationally as we can trace our ancestry. Illegitimate Children are born under the Curse of the Bastard** Deuteronomy 3:2 says "A Bastard shall not enter into the congregation of the Lord; even to his tenth generation shall he not enter into the congregation of the Lord." According to Exodus 20:5-5 we also see that curses can come into the blood-line because of what our forefathers did: Exodus 20:5-6 says "Thou shalt not bow down thyself to them, nor serve them: or I the Lord thy God am a jealous God visiting the iniquity of the fathers upon the children unto the third and fourth generation of them that hate me; And showing mercy unto thousands of them that love me, and keep my commandments. **There are Curses from the New Testament, on those not kind to the needy, Matthew 25: 41-46 On those who refuse the Gospel, Galatians 1:8-9 On those who do not love the Lord, 1 Corinthians 16:22 On those who fall away from Jesus Christ, Hebrews 6:4-8 On all sinners. There are also Self-Inflicted Curses, curses that we pronounce upon ourselves by uttering curses such as, I wish I was dead or wishing some one else dead, when person sys, "damn you" or "damn that" they are in effect pronouncing curses. The practice of sin can expose the believer to curses, we must recognize sin for sin and deal with it recommitting our lives to Jesus and if a curse has been put into place because of sin, then, true repentance must be the starting point of breaking that curse. True repentance is confession of that sin effectively and turning away from that sin.** Curses have to be broken and the demons, spiritual influences and evil spirits that have been allowed to operate have to be cast out, In The Name of Jesus.

Prayer Breaking Any Covenant
Or Agreement with Satan

In the Name of Jesus, Father God, I come to you according to the Word of God and by the power of the Holy Spirit.

Father God, In the Name of Jesus, I repent and tell you that I personally am sorry with a Godly sorrow for having sinned against you.

I ask you Father God to forgive me for my acts of disobedience and rebelliousness that I have enacted against you. I ask you Lord Jesus to forgive me for my sins of ignorance, omission and commission. I renounce them as sin and I declare and decree that this day, I turn away from them.

In the Name of Jesus, I break, cut, sever and loose myself from every covenant, agreement, control, attachments, assignments, contracts, promises, requests made through ignorance, spirits, powers, forces, or lies connect to or made in accordance with any spiritual unions of the Spirit Satan and Evil, that includes Demons, Demonic Influence and Spirit Witches, that also includes any covenants, agreements, rituals, spells, control, attachments, assignments, contracts, promises, requests, spirits, powers, forces, lies, spirit unions of the Spirit Satan, Evil, Demons, Demonic influence, spirit witches made by any of my ancestors, Father or Mother and as far back as Adam on behalf of my blood line.

In The Name of Jesus, I now command the assignments, attachments, covenants, agreements, rituals or spells to be cancelled broken all ungodly soul-ties broken and all Spirits pertaining to those assignments, attachments, covenants, agreements rituals or spells to be bound and to get out of me and my blood-line right now, In The Name of Jesus Christ of Nazareth, Go! Go! Go! All of your works, actions, deeds, thoughts, transference of spirits, spirits sent to over-rule my spirit through soul control Go!
In the Name of Jesus Go!!!!!!!!!!!!!

Prayer Breaking Inheritance Curses

In the Name of Jesus, Father God, I come to you according to the Word of God and by the power of the Holy Spirit. For give my ancestors all the way back to Adam. Forgive us for what happened at the tower of Babel that angered you so much; forgive us for the sins of the world Lust of the eye, Lust of the flesh and the pride of life. Forgive us Lord God for having provided a way and a means for Satan to expand his kingdom.

Right Now, Father God, In the Name of Jesus, I renounce The Spirit Satan, The Spirit of the Anti-Christ, The Spirit of Liar, and The Spirit of Disobedience.
Father God, Right Now, In The Name of Jesus, I break off of me, my family line and everything that concerns us the works, deeds, effects, thoughts and Actions of The Spirit of Satan, The Spirit of Anti-Christ, The Spirit of Liar, The Spirit of Disobedience, The Spirit of The Thief, The Spirit of Death, The Killer Spirit. The Spirit of Dishonor, the Sprit of the Destroyer. Lord God, In the Name of Jesus, I repent for any and all evil we have done in our family line in forsaking the Lordship of Jesus Christ. In the Name of Jesus, I now apply and cover myself, my family and everything that concerns us with a blood covering of the blood of Jesus.

I now renounce all Curses, Confusion, Destruction and Sudden Ruin
Thank you Jesus for dying that I might be made free, Thank you Jesus for becoming a curse that I could have a right to salvation and broken curses.

Jesus I invite you to be Lord of my life, that of my family and especially Lord of my children.

Lord God, I confess that my ancestors and I have sinned and I agree that our sin has been rebellion against the living God. Today Lord Jesus, I ask you to forgive me for my personal sins that have influenced my children.

I ask you Lord Jesus, to set my Children free from any curse on their lives as a result of my sins, especially sins of a worldly nature, Lust of the eye, Lust of the flesh and the pride of Life.

Lord Jesus, I now bring my children to you, and I renounce any and all claims that Satan has put upon my children and my children's children whatever they may be.

In the Name of Jesus and by the shed blood of Jesus Christ, I now nullify every curse of Deuteronomy 27 and 28 and every evil word, deed, thought, effect, or action set charge against me and my blood-line by any spirit, or person living or dead.

Father God, In the Name of Jesus, I ask you to forgive the iniquities and transgressions that have been passed down from generation to generation, as far back as Adam and as far forward as we shall live.

In the Name of Jesus, I bind every demon spirit, evil spirit, unclean spirit, familiar spirit and spirit of bondage. And I command you to release me, my family and everything that concerns me, everything that you have stolen in including my inheritances, finances, lands, homes, title deeds, transportation, relationships, wisdom and knowledge.

In the Name of Jesus, I break your yoke of slavery and I command you to
Get out of me Go!
Go, Right Now In Jesus Name, Go!

Lord God, In The Name of Jesus, I Bless any Human Spirit that is or has in the past been used by Satan to cursed me, my family line and anything that concerns us, In the Name of Jesus And I break the Satanic bondage and demonic hold set charge against them through the trickery of the devil, Lord Jesus, I claim them for your Salvation and eternal life through the cross and the blood of Jesus.

**Fill Those Empty Places
with the Power
of
The Holy Spirit**
Any and all such areas that

**Curses have
Occupied in my life, I ask you Lord Jesus
To fill with the fresh oil and the
Anointing of the Holy Spirit. Fill Me O' God.
Thank you,
Lord Jesus, that you always
Answer my prayers.
Thank You, Holy Spirit**

Spiritual Witchcraft Curses Work

Whether You Believe it or Not,

Just Ask a Witch

Erica Shepherd

It is possible to work Spiritual Witchcraft on someone without them being aware of it? According to the witches, wizards, sorcerers and practitioners, who practice this craft it is. Witchcraft in its simplest form is Unnatural Unauthorized control over others, through the use of natural and supernatural means of sorcery, wizardry, magic, black magic, devil worship, black art, necromancy, witchery, divination, enchantment, spell, bewitchment, Wicca, voodoo, shamanism, diabolism, diablerie, demonology, Satanism; Authoritarian Force. **God says in Leviticus 19:31 Regard not them that have familiar spirits neither seek after Wizards to be defiled by them: I Am the Lord your God. God says in Leviticus 19:26…Neither shall ye use enchantment, nor observe time. The Word of God says in 1 Samuel 15: 23 for rebellion is as the sin of Witchcraft, and stubbornness is as iniquity and idolatry. Deuteronomy 18:10-11 There shall not be found among you anyone that maketh his son or his daughter to pass through the fire, or that useth divination, or an observer of time, or an enchanter, or a Witch, or a charmer, or a consulter with familiar spirits, or a wizard, or a necromancer. For all that do these things are an abomination unto the Lord: Leviticus 20:6-8 And the soul that turneth after such as have familiar spirits, and after Wizards, to go-a-whoring after them, I will even set my face against that soul, and will cut him off from among his people.** Sanctify yourselves therefore, and be ye holy: for I am the Lord your God. And ye shall keep my statutes, and do them: I am the Lord which sanctify you. The first thing that we have to look at is that God says that they exist so we know that Witches are real, what is a Witch, Witchcraft, Wizard and Sorcerer. The Webster's New World College Dictionary, Fourth Ed. Witch, sorcerer, to use magic, to separate (thence set aside for religious worship) 1. A person, esp. a woman, having supernatural power as by a compact with the devil or evil spirits; sorceress. 2. And ugly and ill-tempered old woman: hag; crone 3. A practitioner or follower of white magic or of WICCA, 4. (Informal) a bewitching or fascinating woman or girl. 5. Short for WATER WITCH, to put a magic spell on; bewitch, to charm, Witch-like, Witch'y, Witchier, Wizards, Exodus 22:18Thou shalt not suffer a witch to live **KJV American Standard Version** "*Thou shalt not suffer a sorceress to live.*" **The Answer**: *Put to death any woman who does* **evil magic**. **Amplified Bible**: *You shall not allow a woman to live who practices* **sorcery**. **Good News Version**: *Put to death any woman who practices* **magic**. **James Moffatt Translation**: *You shall not allow any* **sorceress** *to live*. **Jerusalem Bible**: *You shall not allow a* **sorceress** *to live*. **King James Version**: *Thou shalt not suffer a* **witch** *to live*. **Living Bible**: *A* **sorceress** *shall be put to death*. **Modern Language Bible**: *Allow no* **sorceress** *to live*. **New American Bible**: *You shall not let a* **sorceress** *live*. **New American Standard Bible**: *You shall not let a* **sorceress** *live*. **New Century Version**: *Put to death any woman who does* **evil magic**. **New International Version**: *Do not allow a* **sorceress** *to live*. **New Living Translation**: *A* **sorceress** *must not be allowed to live*. **New Revised Standard Version**: *You shall not permit a* **female sorcerer** *to live*. **New World Translation**: *You must not preserve a* **sorceress** *alive*. **The Promise: Contemporary English Version**: *Death is the punishment for* **witchcraft**. **Revised Standard Version**: *You shall not permit a* **sorceress** *to live*. **Revised English Bible**: *You must not allow a* **witch** *to live*. In the original Hebrew manuscript, the author used the word **m'khashepah** to describe the person who should be killed. The word means a woman who uses spoken spells to harm others - e.g. causing their death or loss of property. Clearly *"evil sorceress"* or *"woman who does evil magic"* would be the most accurate phrases in today's English usage for this verse. The *Good News Bible* uses the term *"magic."* **Witches can be both male and female; Priests, Priestesses, Practitioner, Pastor Witches, Bishop Witches, Charismatic Witches, Preacher Witches and Witchcraft: The power or practice of witches, black magic, white magic, an instance of the use of black magic or white magic. Bewitching attraction or charm. Witchdoctor: in certain primitive societies, a person supposed to have the power of curing diseases, warding off evil, through the use of sorcery, incantations, divination, spells, spiritists, mediums, fortune tellers, magic, and enchantments. Witchery: Witchcraft, Sorcery, Bewitching charm, fascination. Witching: the action or practice of a person who witches: witchcraft; that witches; bewitching, there's a lot more just investigate** further for yourself. **A Wizard** is defined as, a sage, a magician, conjurer, sorcerer, a person exceptionally gifted or clever at a specified activity; Wizardry, the art or practice of a wizard, witchcraft, magic, sorcery, exceptional cleverness. **Sorcery** is defined as the use of an evil supernatural power over people and their affairs; black magic seemingly magical power, influence or charm. **Sorcerer a person who practices sorcery, wizard.** So now that we are on the same page let's agree that a Witch is a person who practices Witchcraft, o.k.? White Magic, Black Magic, Sorcery, incantations, necromancy and the like. So then let's agree that it is important for any person to believe in what they are doing and that would include a person practicing witchcraft who from this point on we will call a Witch. Witches believe first that they will not begin to do any witchcraft or what they sometimes refer to as "work " for or on anyone that they don't want their witchcraft stuff to work on, the general witchcraft consensus is white magic will do good and black magic will do bad bringing extreme harm to a person. Sorcery, Necromancy and Wizardry is done for any number of reasons, money, love, power and the like so a lot of people that are sorcerer really don't even believe that they are practicing witchcraft or actually harming anyone with what they do, they call themselves healers, spiritualists and practitioners of the craft, however they are all Witches. And all Witches believe that if there is any doubt as to what they want to befall the person will not happen then they won't do the witchcraft as they believe it will come back directly to them and work against them lessening their ability to perform magic in the future, and bring them shame at their failure in the spiritual world. Witches believe that in order for their witchcraft to work, they must really want and believe it to work and they being to use their will to make it happen (All of this is accomplished within the spiritual realm.) Witches also believe know and understand that their witchcraft will influence those around whom they are working it on, I personally have been a victim of this type of witchcraft many times while in the ministry and casting out demons. In my fight against the demonic and witchcraft the devil very cleverly and deceptively turned the tables on me and called the Gifts of the Holy Spirit, witchcraft and labeled me a Witch. I happened to have been affiliated with a very authoritarian type ministry and I did not yield my will over to the person doing the labeling which happens to have been the Pastor with their own spiritual witchcraft pressure tactics which they were using ignorantly against me. Feeling that they possessed some sort of spiritual ministry superiority over my "John the

Baptist Type, Itinerant Deliverance ministry. The would go about mixing secular and religious positions thinking that they possessed all knowledge of God and how "He works or does not work" substituting carnal knowledge where they lacked Biblical spiritual knowledge of the Holy Spirit gifts of God. Their real concern they were looking for a submissive worker, all the while receiving teaching from what I knew by way of the anointing and experience working to devalue my ministry while expecting me to receive theirs (that is another book). By the way I opened myself up to Demonic incursion because of those encounters. Back to the subject at hand Spiritual Witchcraft is so deceptive and subtle that it will be working on you and against you while you are doing everything that you know of to serve God and that my friend is the very reason that a person is targeted with this type of Witchcraft. Spiritual Witchcraft has the ability to speak sending voices, Spiritual Witchcraft works at reducing your will, and Spiritual Witchcraft can cause you to be infested with unclean spirits that bring in viruses, germs and bacteria to your physical body making you sick, and causing problematic symptoms, actually counterfeiting some real sicknesses with the end result being death. If the witches can they will just out-right kill you, witches can put so much spiritual pressure and weight upon you that you can feel it upon your shoulders, neck, bones and joints. Spiritual Witchcraft can bring so much confusion and manipulation causing a person to make decisions that they know are bad but have no will to resist making them. Spiritual Witchcraft can bring you so much spiritual trouble within your surrounding that you will begin to tire of fighting the spirits of those around you and their families because you know that they are working against you and if you don't fight you will be overtaken by spirits, and that is the real plan of the enemy in the first place he is only using the witches and their witchcraft spirits to bring about your downfall. The Lord Jesus has allowed me to go into Church after Church, home after home, City after city, town after town. Every where I have been sent by The Holy Spirit there has come a point where I have had to overcome Spiritual Witchcraft or leave that place hastily so as not to be overcome by Spiritual witches and spiritual witchcraft, so that I would be able to regroup, get a fresh perspective on what I had just encounter and begin the fight again equipped with more power and knowledge to overcome. Thank God for the blood of Jesus. You see I did not believe in Witchcraft nor did I believe that anyone could do anything to me spiritually that would matter.

I was raised in a good Baptist Home we went to church all the time and the only thing that I knew about anything spiritual was my mother telling me ghost stories as a little girl. Casper the friendly ghost and other comic books, so I thought that it was all fictional we had fortune tellers downtown but I was told that they were gypsies and to not have anything to do with them. It was not until I got saved and filled with the Holy Ghost did I ever hear anything about witches. The first time a lady in the church mentioned a witch I thought she was crazy or something, little did I know how much truth she was trying to relate to me. I found out as these witches were allowed to cross my path by God that different types of witches always brought different types of witchcraft sometimes it was been so bad that I thought I was going to die other times it was so bad that I asked Jesus to take me home because this hell was just to much to bear, or so I thought at that time. I have seen and experienced the bad results of witchcraft and its affects on the families and lives of many people. I have seen witchcraft be instrumental in the break-up of marriages, family relationships, friendships, business relationships churches and church relationships; I have seen the ugliness of death induced by witchcraft. I have seen the devastating results of internet witchcraft, sex witchcraft, elemental witchcraft, necromancy, wizardry and sorcery and the one thing that I have learned about it all is that the end result is always, some sort of death, Spiritual death, Physical death, Mental death or Material death, the really sad thing about all of this Witchcraft is that the Church world and Christians, in particular spirit-filled are not taking it seriously as it sweeps across and is very prevalent in our churches, I know that this is not a very pleasant message or one that people even care to believe and understand however it is very real, dangerous and threatening every day of my life I thank God for his grace and mercy towards me and "His body of believers." The person on whom Spiritual Witchcraft is worked is usually identified by the devil and targeted and their life will be made a living hell. You see Witches know that their witchcraft will permeate around their victim binging out of the spiritual realm the intended harm and torture intended for the targeted person, bringing the harm out of the spiritual realm, into the natural realm thereby, making their intended spoken word curses, spells, jinxes, hexes, vexes, rituals, spells, covenants, contracts, agreements come into effect. They believe that they are using their spiritual power through the working of their will to bring the witchcraft about. Witches also do something called **"owning the enemy" (or the person that they have targeted.)** to put it another way they prevail upon a person in order to get them to yield their will to the will of the witch, wizard, sorcerer or witchcraft spirits, It is will captivation. It is dominating, manipulating and controlling another. Witches will identify a highly anointed person in the church world or any where for that matter, and they will hunt in the secular world for a person who is open to demonic suggestion, many times the person will not be aware that they are being used because they have no conscious knowledge of what they may have inherited or what may have been transferred on them through transference of spirits or demonic soul-ties. Witches, Wizards, and Sorcerers know because they have studied and trained themselves to know, they are power crazed and they want to usurp the spiritual gifting's of the anointed person. Witches know that the best type of person to curse is one open to suggestion and the second best is one that is without knowledge of spiritual operations. Witches know that a spell is any induced condition in which a person's natural and normal self-control over his or her own thinking and actions is usurped, counteracted, controlled, or simply influenced, by some unnatural, exterior force, be it spells or trances regardless of the means, or method by which they are induced mind control, prophecies, that can be self-fulfilling, because of the power of the spoken word and people wanting to believe, they take what is in the Bible and pervert the word of God, because Witches know the Bible is the truth. Witches know and the spirits working with them recognize the anointing of God they know better than the church world the resident power of God within a spirit-filled-individual, so they use the power of the devil and demons to bring their desired results upon a person through supernatural demonic means. The Bible attributes it all to divination. Because of these things the Witches believe that they speak suggestions out of their mouths describing in detail all of the bad things that they spiritually willfully desire to come to pass in the life of heir targeted victim will happen. How so you say? Well the witches believe that the victim will become so entangled with the demonic influences surrounding the victim and if the curses have been spoken directly to the victim that the fear, intimidation, mind control or manipulation will have the victim so caught up in trying to avoid the curse, or the end results of the curse that he or she will end up tripping on unseen demonic obstacles, as they are so distracted by the witch. Whether or not what the witch has predicted will happen to the victim actually happens or not, that doesn't really matter. In the end, they will view it as actually occurring. A self-inflicted hallucination or paranoia. Spiritual witches when they come to a person in the church will make their appearance to the victim in the form of a complete façade. The witches will come as giving caring and concerning; they will use a form of seduction that will appeal to the utmost inner need, of the victim, as they have familiar spirits working in and through them revealing things to them. It is all manipulative and deceitful as they only mean to bring harm. They are spiritual predators that are very much ale to see and recognize the anointing of God upon the life of the spirit-filled person. These Witches have studied the spiritual realm from the perspective of the dark side or satanic realm and are very versed and trained in their chosen craft or mode of operation and the spirits that are working with them have thousands of years worth of experience. Witches also believe that the person claiming, "You can't hurt me with witchcraft, as I am strong in my faith or religious beliefs" and the person that says, "If I don't believe in that stuff, it can't hurt me" are an automatic candidate for them, because there is no resistance or prayer coming against them. Remember behind all witchcraft, witches, wizards, sorcery, divination and bewitchment there are demons and demonic influence at work. I know for a fact that witches are lead by Satan and demons to go into the Churches with the sole purpose of destroying the leadership and the intercessors of the church. Many witches are taught by their leadership how to go into a church and bring spiritual and natural destruction. I have seen and taken many people through exorcisms and deliverance prayers because a witch has dressed the church, the land, the communion wine and a member or two. The churches totally unaware of what was going on, but never the less wondering why people would come and visit the church but would never stay. In one Church in particular the witches prayed psychic prayers and then two of the witches joined forces and actually caused people to become sick. **(I am sure you have heard the expression, you make me sick, well people can have spirits operating within them that can really cause people to become ill.)** You cannot convince a person that has had witchcraft removed and the demons and demonic influence cast-out of them and off of their church buildings and property that Spiritual Witchcraft doesn't exist or work because they know that it did work and I am not talking about the Jezebellic and Ahab type of Spiritual witchcraft. Something ironic, almost unbelievable is the fact that a lot of Christian spiritual witches aren't even aware that they are witches, a lot of them are just doing what they have been taught to do by their grandmothers and mothers to do when they get in a lurch. Many Christian Spiritual witches are working through the psychic gifts that they inherited through birth. Let me give you an example of what happened in a Church that I ran a revival in. Someone practicing voodoo and hoodoo witchcraft had come into the church and taken a bible and an offering tray from the church to work witchcraft through, because they did not like the new pastor. They took those items put them in a plastic bag along with something else meat like and hung it way up in a tree on the property, it was a black plastic bag so it fit right into the tree branches and was not visible, the branches of this tree hung over the parking lot. The Church suffered a decrease in membership, attendance, offerings and new converts went down as well. The Church called for us to come in and run a revival, the Holy Sprit revealed the whole thing, the Gifts of the Holy Spirit working according to 1 Corinthians 12. The articles were found destroyed, the curses broken and the whole church went through Mass Deliverance and Healing. The church returned to normal, people returned to the church and no could give a logical explanation as to why they left in the first place; we know that it was because of the effects of that witchcraft. A male witch is called a "Warlock" but I have not been able to find that word in the Bible, it calls both male and female "Witch." Spiritual Witches and those individual practitioners of the craft can have the ability from Satan to do what is known as soul travel. This is accomplished through out of body experiences they have the supernatural ability to travel and visit a persons home or wherever that person is without the person knowing it unless they choose to make themselves known to you Witches frequently "visit" and spy upon their pray in the form of apparitions and they like to use what they call "tracker and watcher spirits," Have you ever experienced the feeling as if you are being watched in your own home? Have you ever seen what appeared to be small dark little things darting across your floor? How about the appearance of what looked like a pair of eyes staring at you from the corner ceiling of a room? These are just a few of the spiritual tools used in Spiritual Witchcraft there are many more. I had a college professor come for ministry. He came for another problem and found out that another professor at the school where he taught was working Santeria Witchcraft on him in his attempt to knock him out of a promotion, so that the promotion would pass on to him. Santeria is an African-Caribbean witchcraft that was born in Cuba that has legalized animal sacrifice as a part of their religious practice of witchcraft. The closer we get to Jesus' return the more prevalent all types of witchcraft will become. **No one is immune; witches have been known to unloose spirits that have caused people to have fatal car wrecks after having come into contact with them. Witches can unloose spirits that cause people never to be able to keep or build any financial resources, or assets, Witches can unloose spirits upon people that make them appear to be accident-prone and cause them to continually trip, fall and walk into doors and walls for no apparent reason.** It doesn't matter that you don't believe in witchcraft. It only matters that the person who is performing the witchcraft and is knowledgeable about the spiritual realm believes in it and that you don't pray or have any defense against it. No I am not saying that they have more power than God at all. What I am saying is that when Witches are sending out those curses and praying those psychic prayers against you and the church they are in effect causing you and the church stumbling blocks and obstacles by unloosing Evil Spirits and Demonic influences into your personal spiritual atmosphere. Those spiritual forces then will be in effect working against you within the invisible realm of the spirit. The question is what are you doing to protect your spiritual inner man and atmosphere. What are you doing to protect your mind and to protect your body, what type of spiritual warfare are you using. What is your armor, yes God is good and God does protect us, but we have been called to be spiritually responsible as well. We have been called to take some action ourselves, using the authority and operating the power that we have been given by The Lord Jesus Christ and empowered to use by The Holy Spirit. Hundreds of thousands of people are in bondage, caused by the practitioners of Witchcraft, Wizardry, Sorcery, Authoritarian Force and Spiritual Oppression. Within our society today we have religion, within our technological societies and within medicine we have witchcraft and in today's world they are not separate and distinct from one another, many times being commonly interchanged. And when a person has come under its influence until that person is delivered from the willful sin and the effects of its sin, this type of evil spiritual, demonic influence will continue to plague, torment and harass. God's judgment on Babylon recounts, in Isaiah 47:9"…they shall come upon thee in their perfection for the multitudes of thy sorceries, and for the great abundance of thine enchantments." Isaiah 47:1-15 "For thou has trusted in thy wickedness thou hast said, none seeth me, Thy wisdom and thy knowledge, I hath perverted thee; and evil come upon thee; thou shalt not know from whence it riseth; and mischief shall fall upon thee; thou shalt not be able to put it off and desolation shall come upon thee suddenly which thou shalt not know. Stand now with thine enchantments, and with the multitude of thy sorceries, wherein thou has labored from thy youth; of so be thou shalt be able to profit, if so be thou mayest prevail. Thou are wearied in the multitude of thy counsel. Let now the astrologers, the stargazers, the monthly prognosticators, stand up, and save thee from these things that shall come upon thee. Behold they shall be as stubble; the fire shall burn them; they shall deliver themselves from the power of the flame: there shall not be a coal to warm at, nor fire to sit before it. Thus shall they be unto thee with whom thou has labored, even thy merchants from thy youth; they shall wander every one to his quarter; none shall save thee." Colossians 2:6-10 says "As ye have therefore received Christ Jesus the Lord, so walk ye in him: rooted and built up in him, and established in the faith, as ye have been truth, abounding therein with thanksgiving. Beware lest any man spoil you through philosophy and vain deceit, after the tradition of men, after the rudiments of the world, and not after Christ. For in him dwelleth all the fullness of the Godhead bodily. And ye are complete in him (Jesus) which is the head of all principality and power." Matthew 9:6 "But that ye may know that the Son of Man hath power on earth to forgive sins." **All forms of witchcraft are sin. Receiving information from any psychic or occult source is a sin. "This is God's ordinance. Leviticus 19:26-31 "Neither shall ye use enchantment, nor observe times. Regard not them that have familiar spirits, neither seek after wizards to be defiled by them: I Am the Lord. All,** Witchcraft is an abomination to God. Witchcraft is a sinful practice that only brings one thing into the life of a spirit-filled Christian and that is Demonic influence and the indwelling of Evil, Unclean and Familiar spirits of bondage.   1 Cor. 6:19 "What know ye not that your body is the temple of the Holy Ghost which is in you, which ye have of God, and ye are not your own? The Word of God in 1 Thessalonians 5:23 "And the very God of peace sanctify you holly; and I pray God your whole Spirit and Soul and Body be preserved blameless unto the coming of our Lord Jesus Christ." Witchcraft causes our Soul to be lost in hell, curses to come upon our children and the judgment and the wrath of God to come upon our lives. **It is very important that we fast and pray to break Spiritual Witchcraft with its entire works, effects and deeds that may be influencing us, our families, our work places ministries and churches.** Fasting is important to break the yokes of witchcraft. Isaiah 58:6 "Is not this the fast that I have chosen? To loose the bands of wickedness, to undo the heavy burdens, and to let the oppressed go free, and that ye break every (enslaving) yoke?" **Ephesians 6:12 Amplified Bible reads his way, "We wrestle not against flesh and blood, but against despotism's against powers, against (the master spirits who are) the world rulers of this present darkness, against the spirit forces of wickedness in the heavenly (supernatural or spiritual) sphere. But the Lord Jesus Christ did not stop there, in verse 13 we are instructed to put on the whole Armor of God and to stand against the enemy.**

God has given those who believe AUTHORITY over all (devils, demons, witches) over all diseases (spiritual and natural) Jesus, COMMANDED demons, unclean spirits to depart. The recognized His authority and were obedient to Him, Just before He returned to heaven Jesus delegated the same authority to those who believe in His name. This gives the believer the right to use the name of Jesus in making requests to God and in giving commands to demons and to disease. Jesus did not bring us to this point in our walk with God to allow us to be defeated by any witches, Jesus is Lord and Jesus is the one who has anointed and empowered us to do battle and win here on this earthly realm and within the spiritual realm or heavenly realm. **We have been Born-Again to be Victorious in Jesus.**

Prayer Against Witchcraft

This Prayer needs to be Prayed Aloud,

In The Name of Jesus!

Father God, I come to you in the Name of Jesus, by the Word of God and the Power of The Holy Spirit.

In the Name of Jesus, I apply and cover myself, my family and everything that concerns me with a blood covering of the blood of Jesus.

I ask you Lord God, to rebuke in heaven as, I rebuke on earth the Spirit of Witchcraft, Witches, Wizard, Sorcery, Bewitchment, Witchcraft Spirits of Authoritarian Force, Witchcraft Slavery and witchcraft Oppression.

In the Name of Jesus, I now renounce all Witchcraft as sin, and I ask you to forgive me for this sin, whether I have engaged in this sin knowingly or unknowingly.

Lord God, In the Name of Jesus, I ask you for a legion of Angels to assist me in this pray. Warring against the spirits external and airways of Witchcraft, all Transferring Spirits of Witchcraft, all Satanic Working Spirits of Witchcraft summoned up by any members of the Church of Satan On assignment and under contract by witches to work against me and the Holy Spirit and my destiny in Christ Jesus.

In the Name of Jesus, I repent for the sins of my ancestors that may have knowingly or unknowingly opened up me and my family-line to curses due to their involvement whether knowingly, unknowingly or through the sin of ignorance of spiritual witchcraft.

In the Name of Jesus, I break the powers of all curses of witchcraft against me, my family line, my children, my ministry and everything that concerns me. I break your power, words, actions, deeds and effects off me, my ministry, my family, my children, my home, my finances and everything that concerns us I break you off all the way back to Adam.

In the Name of Jesus, I break the power of the Queen of Heaven and renounce any and all control, attachments, assignments; I cancel any and all contracts placed by any person living or dead.

I break any and all blood covenants, agreement, rituals, spells, Oaths, Births, and Death Transference of Spirits through Necromancy agreements.

Any Spirit Transference due to witchcraft untimely death that is working against, hindering, blocking or causing me delay I break your power right now in the Name of Jesus.

In the Name of Jesus, I break every any evil attachments of Witchcraft from any house that I have ever lived in or visited, along with any Church, Ministry or Minister.

In the Name of Jesus, I break the spirits that have been empowered by any Negative Words, Spells or Curses spoken against me, my family line from any past ministries, ministers, Witches, marriages on either side of my family line or that of my spouse.

In the Name of Jesus, and by the Power of the Holy Spirit, I break the power of every Witchcraft Spirit sent by spiritual witchcraft against my life, spouse, family and children against my inheritances, finances, lands, homes and title deeds to be broken right now.

In the Name of Jesus, I break the Spirits of Witchcraft unloosed through covetousness, jealousy, envy, control, domination, manipulation and fear, From this moment on I break the power of all of you spirits name above and any Witchcraft Spirits not named aloud due to my lack of knowing what your name is working against us because you are bound and chained right now in chains covered with a covering of the applied blood of Jesus that I apply to those chains right now never to be unloosed by another human or witchcraft, demonic, satanic or spiritual order.

Angels of God, as these Spirits are bound and Cast-Out carry them to the Pit deposit them there bound and seal it up until the judgment day of Jesus.

In the Name of Jesus I command all Witchcraft Spirits that had been planning and operating against my life, sent by any previous relationship to be bound right now in the Name of Jesus and remain bound as I command you and your effects, strongholds and afflictions to come up along with your roots and your seeds,

In The Name of Jesus and By the Power of The Holy Spirit, I destroy your very works and their influences and every stronghold that abides with witchcraft, domination, manipulation, control, fear and destruction.

In the Name of Jesus, I command you to Go!

Go! Right Now,

Get out, In Jesus Name, Go! And come no more!

Now lift your hands up to God and ask the Lord Jesus, to fill you with freshOil and the Anointing of the Holy Spirit.Fill me Lord Jesus, With the Power of the Holy Spirit Again. Begin to Thank Jesus

Whatever happens in Your Life keep
Thanking God Because of Jesus Christ

1 Thessalonians 5:18 in every thing give thanks: For this is the Will of God,
In Christ Jesus concerning you.

There are many things that are going to come upon you in this life as you endeavor to serve God; you may not understand one half of them. But you can understand this verse of scripture. When bad things happen, give thank to God.
They are sent by the enemy in an attempt to make you doubt the validity of your faith in God.

There is a real enemy, a Spirit enemy the d-evil (devil) who is out to steal our faith, our peace, our love and our joy.

We are commanded in the Word of God, to resist him, this is not easy all the time because he can't be seen and he cleverly disguises his speech, actions, deeds, thought, endeavors and he has the innate ability to make us think it is us, when It is actually him working. The overt things that he does are nothing in comparison with his covert actions.

We are commanded in the Word of God to resist him, staying strong in our faith.

Giving Thanks to God is a powerful way to resist the devil. Even when we do not understand, and it seems like things are out of control and going downhill fast.
Psalms 69:30
I will praise the name of God with a song,
And will magnify him with Thanksgiving

Magnify God by Thanksgiving
Psalm 100:4
Enter into "His" gates with Thanksgiving, and into
"His" courts with praise, be thankful unto "Him" and
Bless "His" Name
Enter Gods gate with thanksgiving.

Psalm 75:1
Unto thee, O God, do we give Thanks, unto thee do we
Give Thanks
For thy Name is near thy wondrous works declare

Romans 6:17
But God be Thanked, that ye were the servants of sin, but
Ye have obeyed from the heart that form of doctrine which
Was delivered you.

**Force yourself by an Act of your will to
Thank God for what "He" is doing, for what "He" has done in the past
And for what you know by "Faith" that "He" is going to do for you.
No Matter what may be happening**

1 Thessalonians 5:18 LB
No Matter what happens, Always be Thankful for this is God's
Will for you who belong to Christ Jesus.

Say This Aloud

**I will keep Thanking God
No Matter What Happens
Now Thank God
Let Thanksgiving arise up out of your
Heart until it reaches Our Father In Heaven**

Prayer to break Prayerlessness and

Spiritual Slackness Paul Cox, Aslan's place

Father God, in the name of Jesus, I shut every demonic door that has been opened to hinder my prayer life. I bind the cares of the world and the pride of life. Leviathan is bound from my neck and Behemoth has no place in my loins. Pride and deception are my enemies and not my friends. I break every dark covenant that has been set against the call of God on my life. I am liberated from every unholy thing that would creep into the corridors of my spiritual life. I renounce all soul ties that would distract my mind from my prayer assignment. I bind all financial, emotional, physical, associational, and professional distractions against my private time with God and my prayer assignment on the wall. I renounce any witchcraft or forms of manipulation that would infiltrate my spiritual life. The spirit of infirmity is bound; the spirit of slumber is bound; the spirit of slothfulness is bound; the spirit of hopelessness is bound. Greed and selfishness are bound forever off of me. I am quickened by the Spirit of the

Most High God to Fast, Watch and Pray, Worship,

Study the Word and do Warfare in the Name of Jesus.

The spiritual discipline of the Lord is my portion. The lines of the spirit have fallen upon me to stand in the gap. I get in my place called there and position myself on the wall. I break off of me, my ministry and the call of God upon my life, the spirits of Sanballat and Tobiah. I say I will not come down off the wall. I am doing a great work for the Lord! Lord, show me any people, places or things that have been strategically put in my path to blind my eyes, close my ears and shut my mouth in the spirit. I plead the blood of Jesus over my eyes, ears, and mouth. They will be used by God in this hour. I renounce outright and subliminal idolatry that might be affecting me. I am not my own and I do not lean to my own understanding. My spiritual life is prosperous and no good thing will be held back from me. Everything that I put my hands to the plow to do is blessed. The blessings of the Lord are running me down and taking me over. I am in my coast and my enemies have no power to stand against me, in the matchless name of Jesus I pray, Amen.

Prayer of release into financial freedom

I repent that I have not treated and valued the Kingdom of Heaven as I should and that I have exchanged the value of the Kingdom of Heaven for the desires of my heart in the form of earthly Kingdom. Lord I repent for worrying about life, food, and clothing. I repent for laying up treasures on earth where moths and rust destroy and where thieves break in and steal. I repent for robbing the Lord and not freely and cheerfully giving my offerings to you out of a heart of love.

Lord I repent for loving money, for serving Mammon (riches), for greed and for covetousness.

I repent of the belief that money is the answer to everything in my life. I repent of expecting money to be my answer and my friend. I repent for forsaking you as my life source and for focusing my eyes on the pursuit of wealth to my own harm and the harm of others. I repent for choosing to serve Mammon in preference to you and thereby filling my life with darkness. I renounce on behalf of my ancestors and myself for every agreement made with Mammon by using money in ungodly ways and for ungodly purposes. I repent for being double-minded with money and unstable in all of my ways. I choose to hate Mammon and love you Lord with my whole heart. I choose to place my treasure where my heart is, in the Kingdom of Heaven, for you to use as you choose.

I repent for making money my defender, security and protection.

I repent for believing that chants, spells, fate, superstition, and luck will provide the money I need.

I repent for myself and my family line for using diverse weights and measures and not paying our employees their due.

I repent for making money the center of the universe and not You, Lord.

I repent for pride, gaining wealth by dishonest means and vain striving for silver and gold. I repent for myself and my family line for not exercising my responsibility to pay money that was owed to the governmental agencies. I repent for defrauding, cheating, lying and stealing from the government. I also repent for a begrudging and bitter attitude in paying my taxes. I repent for not recognizing your anointing on government to provide for the basic necessities of our corporate life together. I repent for criticizing, complaining and cursing my government for not providing enough for the people.

I repent for myself and my generational line for seeking, accepting, treasuring, profiting from, and spending blood money. I also repent for adding blood money to my children's inheritance. On behalf of my ancestors, I choose to forgive those financial institutions which have foreclosed on mortgages and stolen property which rightfully belonged to me and my descendants as an inheritance.

I repent across my generational line for abandoning and sacrificing family and relationships, land and culture and even faith in God and for seeking gold and earthly treasures. I choose to seek after the ultimate treasure of my Lord Jesus Christ with all my heart.

I repent on behalf of myself and my ancestors for believing in a poverty mindset and being stingy with the body of Christ. I declare that Jesus came to give us abundant life. Father, in your mercy free me and my future generations of the consequences of this. I repent and confess the lie that godliness implies poverty, lacking in basic necessities, living in poverty, always being in need, and that the children would never procure their education. I choose to believe and accept that God will supply all of my needs and that there will be an inheritance for a thousand generations that my descendants will not have to beg for food and that all my needs will be met.

I repent for being disconnected from the River of Life of God's endless supply. I choose to be connected to the River of Life where God will grant me the ability to acquire wealth for His Kingdom. I repent for spending money on that which does not satisfy and not coming to your living waters to drink.

I repent for myself and my generational line for hardening my heart and shutting my hand against my poorer brothers in their needs. I repent of holding back my possessions and services to get higher prices from those in need. I declare I will open my hand and heart to the poor, sharing my resources as You lead so no one will lack and Your power will not be hindered and Your grace will remain. I repent for spending money on that which does not satisfy and not coming to your living waters to drink and bringing unity in the Body of Christ. I choose to not hold back from the needy. I break in Jesus name the curses that have come against me and my generational line for demanding unfair prices from the needy. Lord would you release your blessings and grace on my selling and trading, especially to those in need.

I repent for not feeding the poor nor taking care of the widows and orphans.

I repent for myself and my family line for not receiving the inheritance that you had for us and I choose to receive the inheritance, abundance and gifts that you have for us. I ask that it will come in such abundance that we will be able to leave an inheritance for our children and grandchildren.

Lord I ask you to disconnect my ancestors, me, and my descendants from money that was tied to freemasonry, secret societies, secret agendas, covert operations, ungodly funding of churches and institutions and for the building of ungodly altars and for funding prostitutes.

Lord break off the curse of sowing much and bringing in little, eating and not having enough, and earning wages only to put them into a bag with holes.

Lord I ask you to destroy the connectors and cleanse the ley lines attached between me and earthly treasures.

Lord, connect me to you alone. I choose not to hold on to anything but you. I give everything I have to you.

I repent for myself and my family line for the judgment that the gifts of the Holy Spirit could be purchased or sold. I break the curse that the money in my generational line and in my life would perish with me. I repent for my wickedness and my generational wickedness and ask that my heart would be restored into a right relationship with you.

Lord I repent for making my giving an obligation to you and not a free act of my love. Lord remove the yoke of obligation from me. Remove the canopy of law and obligation from me. Lord allow me to live in your grace and your provision.

I ask you Holy Spirit to be the One who directs me what to give. Lord make my giving come from an attitude of gratitude and of love. I choose to seek and follow your guidance in my giving.

Lord I repent for not trusting you and not trusting you to provide.

On behalf of my ancestors and myself and for future generations, I choose to forgive those who have swindled me, especially banks and financial institutions, and government agencies, and those who have charged me usury, and those who have tried to keep me in poverty and have disinherited my children.

I declare I will be content in you and in my wages in whatever financial state I am in.

Lord thank you for giving me the creativity to produce wealth in seed. Holy Spirit teach me what to sow, what to reap, and what to harvest for your purpose.

I declare that I will eat of the bread of life and delight in your abundance.

I declare that I am one member of many members of the body of Christ in whom are all the hidden treasures of wisdom and knowledge.

Lord would you please release into me the blessing and joy of giving freely in accordance with Your will for my life.

Lord help me to see money with spiritual eyes, knowing it is Your resource and it belongs to You. Lord would you release the treasures that the enemy has stolen from me and my family line.

I declare that your Word says: you will go before us and make the crooked places straight; I will break in pieces the gates of bronze and cut the bars of iron. You will give us the treasures of darkness and hidden riches of secret places. You are the One who gives power to get wealth that you may establish your covenant which you swore to our fathers, as it is this day. The blessing of the LORD makes *one* rich, and you add no sorrow with it. The generous soul will be made rich, and he who waters will also be watered himself. Thank you for enabling me to leave an inheritance to my children's children.

Lord would you give me a circumcised heart so you can release your treasure from heaven.
Genesis 8:22
Deuteronomy 8:18; 10:16; 15:7-8
Psalm 62:6
Proverbs 10:22; 11:25-26; 13:10-11, 22; 13:22, 18; 1120:13
Eccl 5:10, 7:12, 10:19
Isaiah 45:1-3, 55:1-2
Haggai 1:5-6
Matthew 6:21; 13:44-66; 19-24; 22:19-22; 27:6
Luke 3:14
Luke 12:22-23
Acts 4:32-35; 8:18-24
I Corinthians 12:12
II Corinthians 8, 9
I Timothy 3:2-3, 6:10
Hebrews 13:5
Revelation 3:17-18

Prayer to release me in to my
God Given Influence, Paul Cox Aslan's place

I choose to forgive those that have come against my spiritual authority and influence. I forgive those that declared that I was not operating in the Spirit because they want to restrict me to a dimension of their understanding in the natural realm. I forgive them for coming against the influence that you chose for me to have. I choose to forgive those who have suppressed woman and children and limited their potential for growth. I forgive those who have silenced women and children and placed over women and children barriers that have hindered them from coming into their destiny. Lord, forgive me and my ancestors for suppressing, limiting, silencing, and hindering women and children from their destiny.

I repent for myself and for those in my generational line who have limited authority to those who express themselves logically and have shut out those who express themselves emotionally, intuitively, and through their spiritual giftings.
I ask now, Jesus, that you bring my wheel of influence into proper balance, put the spokes back into place, repair the rim, and repair all the dings and damage. Lord would you remove all influence of ungodly elders.

Lord please put the hub in the right place and center it in Jesus Christ. I am choosing to be in the center of Jesus' will and only have the influence that Jesus wants me to have. And Lord would you remove any evil attack against the wheel, and align the wheel to your kingdom purposes. Lord would you place the anointing that you want me to have on the hub. Lord would you destroy any birds, especially ravens that would seek to attack this wheel and the influence you want me to have. Lord would bring the speed of the wheel back into balance. Lord would you bring the wheel back into right alignment within the dimensions and within time. I demand that Kronos get off my wheel. Lord, would you release your power on this wheel. Lord may the wheel only operate under your power, not mine or the enemy's. I draw strength only from you. I choose to have my influence to be totally guided by you and affected by you. If, Lord, in any way, the wheel is out of control or other people are trying to control my wheel. Lord would You break that off. I declare again that my Godly influence will only be affected by You. I demand all man-fearing spirits to leave, all co-dependency to leave, manipulation to leave and control to leave.

Live Long And Strong

DEUTERONOMY 34:7 NIV

7 Moses was a hundred and twenty years old when he died, yet
his eyes were not weak nor his strength gone.
Old age should not be a time to dread. We can look to God and
receive strength, health, and provision for a full and enjoyable life.
God's plan for you is NOT an old age full of sickness, poverty,
and loneliness. Moses and Joshua are examples for us.

JOSHUA 14:10-11 NKJ

10 "And now, behold, the Lord has kept me alive, as He said,
these forty-five years, ever since the Lord spoke this word to
Moses while Israel wandered in the wilderness; and now, here I
am this day, eighty-five years old.
11 "As yet I am as strong this day as on the day that Moses
sent me; just as my strength was then, so now is my strength
for war, both for going out and for coming in.

GALATIANS 3:13-14 NKJ

13 Christ has redeemed us from the curse of the law, having
become a curse for us (for it is written, "Cursed is everyone
Who hangs on a tree"),
14 that the blessing of Abraham might come upon the Gentiles in
Christ Jesus, that we might receive the promise of the Spirit through faith.
Galatians 3 tells us we are to receive the blessing of Abraham
-- through faith -- because of what Jesus has done. Now, read

the following verses about Abraham.

GENESIS 13:2 NKJ
2 Abram was very rich in livestock, in silver, and in gold.

GENESIS 25:8 NASB
8 And Abraham breathed his last and died in a ripe old age, an
old man and satisfied with life;
And he was gathered to his people.
Because Jesus has redeemed us from the curse, we also should
believe God for a long, enjoyable, and productive life. And we
should resist the devil who would try to steal it away from us.
We have the promise of God that He will satisfy us with life.
(If you are not satisfied with your life, make some changes.
God intends for you to be satisfied.)

PSALM 91:16 NKJ
16 with long life I will satisfy him, and show him my
salvation."

PSALM 103:5 NKJ
5 who satisfies your mouth with good things, So that your youth is renewed
Like the eagle's.
God made our bodies to repair and renew themselves. As we walk
and talk in faith, looking to the promises of God, the life of
God will renew our bodies. (We should also allow God to guide
us in the things we take into our bodies -- only putting good things
Into our mouths.)

PSALM 92:14 NKJ
14 They shall still bear fruit in old age; They shall be fresh
and flourishing,

ISAIAH 46:4 NIV
4 Even to your old age and gray hairs I am he, I am he who will
sustain you. I have made you and I will carry you; I will
sustain you and I will rescue you.
God is faithful. He will always be our wonderful Father, our
great Provider, Helper, and Healer -- no matter how old we are,
Or what we face.

The Spirits Are Subject Unto You
Jesus has redeemed me from the curse, so I will live a
long, victorious, overcoming enjoyable life to the glory of God.

List of Demons
From "Pigs in the Parlor
Frank and Ida Mae Hammond

BITTERNESS - resentment, hatred, unforgiveness, violence, temper, anger, retaliation, murder

REBELLION - self-will, stubbornness, disobedience, anti-submissiveness

STRIFE - contention, bickering, argument, quarreling, fighting

CONTROL - possessiveness, dominance, witchcraft

RETALIATION - destruction, spite, hatred, sadism, hurt, cruelty

ACCUSATION - judging, criticism, faultfinding

REJECTION - fear of rejection, self-rejection

INSECURITY - inferiority, self-pity, loneliness, timidity, shyness, inadequacy, ineptness

JEALOUSY - envy, suspicion, distrust, selfishness

WITHDRAWAL - pouting, daydreaming, fantasy, pretension, unreality

ESCAPE - indifference, stoicism, passivity, sleepiness, alcohol, drugs

PASSIVITY - indifference, listlessness, lethargy

DEPRESSION - despair, despondency, discouragement, defeatism, dejection, hopelessness, suicide, death, insomnia, morbidity

HEAVINESS - gloom burden disgust

WORRY - anxiety, fear, dread, apprehension

NERVOUSNESS - tension, headache, nervous habits, restlessness, excitement, insomnia, roving

SENSITIVENESS -- self-awareness, fear of man, fear of disapproval

PERSECUTION - unfairness, fear of judgment, fear of condemnation, fear of accusation, fear of reproof, sensitiveness

MENTAL ILLNESS - insanity, madness, mania, retardation, senility, schizophrenia, paranoia, hallucinations

PARANOIA - jealousy, envy, suspicion, distrust, persecution, fears, confrontation, forgetfulness

DOUBT - unbelief, skepticism

INDECISION - procrastination, compromise, confusion, forgetfulness, indifference

SELF-DECEPTION - self-delusion, self-seduction, pride

MIND-BINDING - confusion, fear of man, fear of failure, occult spirits, Spiritism spirits

MIND IDOLATRY - intellectualism, rationalization, pride, ego

FEARS (ALL KINDS) - phobias (all kinds), hysteria

FEAR OF AUTHORITY - lying, deceit

PRIDE - ego, vanity, self-righteousness, haughtiness, importance, arrogance

AFFECTATION - theatrics, playacting, sophistication, pretension, drama

COVETOUSNESS - stealing, kleptomania, material lust, greed, discontent

PERFECTION - pride, vanity, ego, frustration, criticism, irritability, intolerance, anger

COMPETITION - driving, argument, pride, ego, (having to be better than your neighbor in any way, shape, or form)--added by Issachar Prophet

IMPATIENCE -- agitation, frustration, intolerance, resentment, criticism

FALSE BURDEN - false responsibility, false compassion

GRIEF - sorrow, heartache, heartbreak, crying, sadness, cruel

FATIGUE - tiredness, weariness, laziness

INFIRMITY - (may include any disease or sickness)

DEATH

INHERITANCE - physical, emotional, mental, curses

HYPER-ACTIVITY - restlessness, driving, pressure

CURSING - blasphemy, course jesting, gossip, criticism, backbiting, mockery, belittling, railing, (La' Shan hara, speaking forth Satan's kingdom in any way, shape, or form)--added by Issachar Prophet

ADDICTIVE AND COMPULSIVE - nicotine, alcohol, drugs, medications, caffeine, gluttony

GLUTTONY - nervousness, compulsive eating, resentment, frustration, idleness, self-pity, self-reward

SELF-ACCUSATION - self-hatred, self-condemnation

GUILT - condemnation, shame, unworthiness, embarrassment

SEXUAL IMPURITY - lust, fantasy lust, masturbation, homosexuality, lesbianism, adultery, fornication, incest, harlotry, rape, exposure, frigidity

CULTS - Jehovah's Witnesses, Christian Science, Rosicrucian's, Theosophy, Urantia, Subud, Latihan, Unity, Mormonism, Bahaism, Unitarianism, (Lodges, societies and social agencies using the Bible and God as a basis, but omitting the blood atonement of Yeshua HaMaschiah)

OCCULT - Ouija board, palmistry, handwriting analysis, automatic handwriting, ESP, hypnotism, horoscope, astrology, levitation, fortune telling, water witching, Tarot cards, pendulum, witchcraft, black magic, white magic, conjuration, incantation, charms, fetishes, etc.

RELIGIOUS - ritualism, formalism, legalism, doctrinal obsession, seduction, doctrinal error, fear of Hell, fear of lost salvation, religiosity, etc.

SPIRITISM - séance, spirit guide, necromancy, etc.

FALSE RELIGIONS - Buddhism, Taoism, Hinduism, Islam, Shintoism, Confucianism, etc.

I Timothy 4:1-2 says: Now the Spirit expressly says that in latter times some will depart from the faith, giving heed to deceiving spirits and doctrines of demons, (which is always anti-Torah or anti-Christ, however you want to say it, it's the same.) speaking lies in hypocrisy, having their own conscience seared with a hot iron.

James 4:4 says: Adulterers and adulteresses!

Be on the Watch for Spirits to Manifest in These areas
  By: Apostle Ivory L. Hopkins
    Satan's Hit List

  1.   Unexpected trouble in the family that you never expected.

2. Sickness and disease all of a sudden to slow you down or kill you.

3. Problems so confusing that you blame your self and those around you.

4. Confusion of the mind and surroundings not knowing who to blame.

5. Financial attacks out of seemingly know where.

6. Things breaking down keeping you upset (automatic failure)

7. Arguments among yourselves that doesn't make since.

8. Children doing crazy stuff at the worse possible moment

9. Strong trials that make a person feel like backsliding and cuts close at hand what would pull you in.

10. Relatives manifesting on you with dumbest foolishness you ever heard of.

11. Trouble on the job that God gave you making you doubt who gave you the job.

12 Close friends making you feel worse when you are already going through. (Jobs Friends)

13. Feeling of depression and suicide in order to take you out.

14 Intense feelings of dread and stress with no identifiable source.

15 Making small problems bigger then what they are.
    (Where there is no problem he creates one where there is a problem he blows it up).

16. Causing you to manifest your worst canal weakness possible in front of people,
    Making you hate yourself instead of seeking God for grace over it.

17. Hearing backbiting about you that makes you want to quit church and go back in the world.

18. Temptations increasing when you finally decide to come out of a certain sin.

19. Pastors with something going in the congregation making you wonder if you are
    The right one to pastor the church.

20. PK'S (Pastors Kids) see things out of church people making them never want to be a pastor or can't wait until their old enough not to go to church.

21. Making members constantly feeling like leaving the church for no reason at all or one Satan sets up in order to stop that body from having who and what they need to finish God's vision for the house.

Spiritual Warfare Booklist

1. Demons And Deliverance H.A. Maxwell Whyte

2. Casting out Demons H.A. Maxwell Whyte

3. Demon Hit List, Prayers to Rout Demons, John Eckhardt

4. Guide to Spiritual Warfare E. M. Bounds

5. Demons--The Answer Book Lester Sumerall

6. Deliverance from Evil Spirits Francis McNutt

7. Deliverance and Inner Healing John Sandford

8. Occult Bondage and Deliverance Kurt Koch

9. Generational Deliverance Paul Cox

10. Deliver Us from Evil Don Basham

11. Silencing the Enemy Robert Gay

12. How to Cast Out Demons Doris M. Wagner

13. Healing Through Deliverance Peter Horrobin

14. They Shall Expel Demons Derek Prince

15. Spiritual Warfare Derek Prince

16. The Beautiful Side of Evil Yohanna Michaelsen

17. Pigs In The Parlor Frank and Ida Mae Hammond

18. Blessing Or Curse--You Can Choose Derek Prince

19. Kingdom Living For the Family Frank Hammond

20. Saints at War Frank Hammond

21. Deliverance Manual Gene Moody

22. Can A Christian Have A Demon? Don Basham

23. The Bondage Breaker Neil T. Anderson

24. Spiritual Warfare Richard Ing

25. Power of The Blood H.A. Maxwell Whyte

26. Discerning Of Spirits Francis Frangipane

27. The Three Battlegrounds Francis Frangipane

28. Deliver Us from Evil Cindy Jacobs

29. The Jezebel Spirit Francis Frangipane

30. Breaking Generational Curses Marilyn Hickey

31. Apostle Kimberly Daniels, Clean House Strong House, Take it back,
32. Alice Smith and Eddie Smith, Delivering the Captives
33. Peter Horrobin, Deliverance and Healing
34. The Mask of the Demon, Wallen Yep
35. Apostle Ivory L. Hopkins
36. Bishop T. D. Jakes
37. Paul and Eve Fernandez, Trauma
38. Paul Cox, Generational Deliverance, Many others books on Discernment and Deliverance
40. God, The Holy Bible

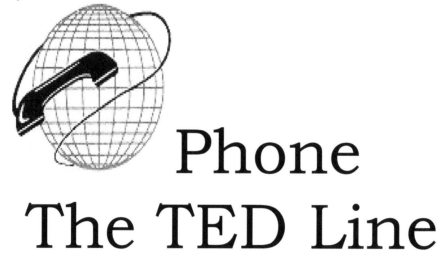

Phone
The TED Line

The Ted Line
Free
Live
Telephone Exorcism
Deliverance
Sunday Nights, U.S.A.
First Sunday of Every Month
9:00pm
Call 1-877-230-1110
For Number

Integrated Healing Prayer Ministry
Phone the TED Line
Email
Erica@phonethetedline.com
phoneted@msn.com
Websites:
www.integratedhealingprayerministry.com
www.phonethetedline.com
www.aladyexorcist.com
1-877-230-1110
1-344-460-9972